Praying Through the Bible

Volume 1: Genesis–Joshua

Selected Books by Markus McDowell

Praying Through the Bible. Volume 2: Judges–Second Samuel

Prayers of Jewish Women: Studies of Patterns of Prayer in the Second Temple Period

Prayer in the Ancient Stoic Tradition: With a Comparison to Prayers of the New Testament

Epistolary Prayer in the Apostolic Fathers

The Practice of Prayer: The Character of Prayer

Let the Bible Speak: A Simple, Three-Part Method for Bible Study

The Prayers of Genesis

The Prayers of Exodus

The Prayers of Leviticus and Numbers

The Prayers of Deuteronomy

The Prayers of Joshua

Praying Through the Bible

Volume 1: Genesis–Joshua

SECOND EDITION

Markus McDowell

Los Angeles | London
www.SulisInternational.com

Published by Sulis International
Los Angeles | London
www.sulisinternational.com

Join the Sulis mailing list at http://bit.ly/2idrJxN

Book design by Sulis International

Copyright ©2017 by Markus McDowell
Second Edition

All rights reserved. No part of this publication may be reproduced in any form by any means without permission from the publisher, except for the inclusion of brief quotations in a review.

Library of Congress Cataloging-in-Publication Data is available.
ISBN 978-0692576519
1. Religion 2. Christian Life 3. Prayer

All Scripture quotations, unless otherwise noted, are from the New Revised Standard Version of the Bible, copyrighted, 1989 by the Division of Christian Education of the National Council of the Churches of Christ in the United States of America, and are used by permission. All rights reserved.

*To my little sister Jackie
for her steadfastness, strength, and love.*

Table of Contents

Table of Contents 9
Preface to the Second Edition..1
Introduction 3
Studying the Bible 11
The Types of Prayers..19

Genesis..41
   Introduction 43
   The Personal Name of God (Gen 4.26) 45
   Noah's Blessings and Curses (Gen 9.25-27).....................51
   Melchizedek Blesses Abram (Gen 14.19-20)....................55
   Abraham Intercedes for Abimelech (Gen 20.7, 17) 59
   Hagar's Lament and Petition (Gen 21.16)........................63
   A Chain of Prayers (Gen 24.12-14, 27, 42-44, 48,
   52, 60)...67
   Intercession and Petition for a Child (Gen 25.21, 22).....73
   A Blessing Wrought in Deception (Gen 27.7, 12–13,
   27–29; 28.2-4) 77
   Jacob's Vow (Gen 28.20-22) 83
   Waiting in Prayer (Gen 30.17-22) 89
   Jacob's Petition for Safety (Gen 32.9-12) 93
   Israel's Prayer for His Son's Success (Gen 43.14)..........99
   Israel Blesses the Sons of Joseph (Gen 48.15-16, 20)...103
   A Brief Prayer of Trust in God by Jacob (Gen 49.18) ..107
   Summary of the Prayers in Genesis................................111

Exodus 113
   Introduction 115
   The Israelites Cry Out for Help (Exod 2.23) 117
   Moses Offers a Prayer on Behalf of Pharaoh
   (Exod 8.8-9, 12) 123
   Moses Prays Again for the Pharaoh
   (Exod 9.28-29, 33) 129
   Moses Offers a Third Prayer for the Pharaoh (Exod
   10.17-18) 133
   A Prayer-Hymn of Praise (Exod 15.1-18) 139
   Miriam and the Women Praise God (Exod 15.21) 145
   Jethro Blesses the Lord (Exod 18.10) 149
   Summary of the Prayers in Exodus 155

Leviticus 157
   Leviticus 159
   Aaron Blesses the People (Lev 9.22) 163
   Summary of the Prayer in Leviticus 167

Numbers 169
   Introduction 171
   The Lord Bless You and Keep You (Num 6.24-26) 173
   The Song of the Ark (Num 10.35-36) 179
   The Art of Complaining (Num 11.2) 183
   Prayers, Whiners, and Snakes (Num 21.7) 189
   Men, Daughters, Wives and Vows (Num 30) 193
   Summary of the Prayers in Numbers 199

Deuteronomy 203
   Introduction 205
   Praying for More (Deut 1.11) 207
   Perspective in Fear (Deut 3.24-25) 211
   Do Not Forget (Deut 8.10) 215
   Extreme Prayer (Deut 9.26-29) 221
   A Prayer for First Fruits (Deut 26.13-15) 225
   Four Kinds of Blessings (Deut 33.6-29) 231
   Summary of the Prayers in Deuteronomy 239

Table of Contents

Joshua	243
Introduction	245
A Not-Prayer (Joshua 1.17)	249
A Curse-Prayer (Joshua 6.26)	255
A Lament (Joshua 7.7–9)	261
A Weak Confession (Joshua 7.20–21)	267
A Failure To Pray (Joshua 9.14)	273
A Secularized Prayer (Joshua 10.12)	277
Blessings (Joshua 14.13, 22.6–7)	283
Summary of the Prayers in Joshua	287
Conclusion	289
Appendix Prayers by Category	291
ABOUT THE AUTHOR	295

Preface to the Second Edition

This new edition of *Praying Through the Bible, Volume 1: Genesis–Joshua*, includes a number of improvements. First, some typographical and formatting errors have been corrected, thanks to my readers and reviewers. Second, I have rewritten some sections for better readability. Third, I have divided each chapter into three parts: a "background" section, a "meaning" section, and an "application" setting. I began using this structure as I wrote the second volume, and my early readers and editors said it was much more helpful for study and use.

I thank my reviewers and beta readers, along with the editors at Sulis International. Without them, this book would never have been finished. Their insights and critiques are invaluable.

I thank all my readers for the success of the first edition, and I hope and pray that this second edition will continue to help people enrich their prayers and serve others.

Finally, thank you to my wife, a constant source of strength and model of perseverance and success. I cannot thank God enough for you, my love.

Markus McDowell
Paso Robles, California
13 January 2017

Introduction

Many of us who pray sometimes feel that our prayers could be better. We might wish we prayed more often, or wish that the words of our prayers were better (whatever that might mean). Maybe we wonder if we are praying the "wrong" things. Of course, we should know that, since God is our Father, He is pleased if we talk to Him at all—even badly.

Still, many of us wish we felt more engaged when we pray. Our prayers can seem rote, distant, or missing *something*. Often, that "something" is a lack depth, richness, or variety. We find ourselves saying the same things in the same way. Most of us never had anyone that taught us how to pray—we just mimicked what we heard from others. We yearn for a way to enrich our prayers and add variety and depth.

After more than twenty-five years of studying prayer, both on own and while earning my degrees, I still cannot say that I understand it. No one can, because prayer is, to a certain extent, a mystery. It is an ongoing conversation with the Divine, the Creator of the Universe. That does not mean, however, that we cannot learn and grow in our understanding and practice of prayer.

Scripture is a good place to begin. There are hundreds of prayers, teachings about prayer, and mentions of prayer. As I began studying them, I found a richness and variety that I had not noticed before. I saw new possibilities for prayer in their content, structure, times, and types.

It occurred to me that, if I could study every mention prayer in the Bible, not only would I learn a lot, but it would also enrich my own prayers. What better resource than God's word?

In 2011, I began working on a project I called "Praying Through the Bible." I been writing and speaking about prayer for many years before that, and had many hundreds of people tell me that they would like to enrich their prayer life, too. So I began the project as a blog, with the first mention of prayer in the Bible.[1] During the next few years, I worked my way through each prayer in Genesis, then Exodus, and so on. The blog gained popularity and attracted followers all over the world. My own understanding of prayer grew through comments and emails from my readers. Many asked me for a book of these studies—something they could use for personal and group study and devotion. I edited, expanded, and revised the entries into a "devotional commentary"—a Bible study with practical application. The result is the book you are reading now: the first volume of *Praying Through the Bible*.

---

[1] See "The Personal Name of God (Gen 4.26)."

Introduction

The Purpose of This Book

The goal of this book is to study the prayers of the Bible and use them as models for our own prayers. Each chapter examines a passage that contains a prayer, mentions prayer, or teaches about prayer. Sometimes it is only one verse or a part of a verse; sometimes it covers many verses. I have kept together prayer passages that belong together. For example, if a character says they are going to pray, then prays, and then mentions it later, that is the subject of one entry (chapter).

Each chapter contains three parts: a study of the passage, exploration of the prayer within that passage, and what we can learn from it. As noted above, this book is a "devotional commentary," which means that its primary purpose is spiritual application. To meet that goal with care, we will seek to understand each passage within the context of its section and book. Since the Bible was written in ancient times, we will also look at the historical context when helpful. Likewise, we'll look at some cultural aspects that might help us understand that ancient culture. If relevant, we will examine the original language used or a literary technique. Anything that helps us understand the prayer passage is fair game.

Once we have a sound understanding of the prayer in its context, we can explore how the original readers might have read it. We will also consider how the writer might have understood it. After that, we are ready to making some suggestions about how that prayer can be used to enrich our prayers.

I have attempted to keep every chapter short, to make it easy to read one passage at a sitting, and for use as a daily devotional or a group study. Some passages need more exploration than others, of course. For the longer passages, I have broken up the study into several chapters.

How to Use This Book

I offer two suggestions for using this book. First, read the prayer itself at least once, and perhaps more. You might even read it out loud. Refer to the words of the prayer as you read through the chapter. I have included the text of each prayer at the beginning of each chapter. If you want even more depth in your study, read the chapter or chapters of the Bible from which the prayer came.

Second, I recommend using a prayer journal or notebook to keep track of what you learn and your practice of prayer. In some chapters, I suggest writing a prayer or specific notes. Prayer is an action, part of our relationship with our Creator. Just reading about it is not enough for full growth. We need to *do* it, to practice what we learn. At the end of each chapter, there are suggestions as to how to incorporate what we learn into your prayers. Of course, you are free to ignore any of these suggestions and do what works best for you. But I do encourage you to put into immediate practice what we study in each chapter.

The book begins with the first prayer in Genesis and continues through to the last prayer in Joshua. Later volumes will cover the rest of the Old and New Testament until we reach the final prayer of the book of Revelation. As you read this book, it is best to begin with the first prayer and continue in order, because we will build on what we learn as we go along. However, the book is still useful if you dip into a chapter here and there (perhaps you have an interest in a particular book of the Bible or a particular character). The book includes an appendix of prayer types for that purpose. Each chapter can stand on its own, although you will miss the fuller context and previous understandings.

Most of the chapters address one prayer and one type of prayer. Some contain multiple types. Practice each type after each chapter. It may seem a bit artificial to pray *only* thanksgiving prayers for a while, but doing so will immerse you in that form of prayer, and, along with the study of the prayer, you will have a good practical foundation to use it more naturally. You will find some types more comfortable than others, and that is okay—but don't forget to stretch yourself by trying them all. Pushing ourselves beyond our comfort level is how we grow.

Though I describe the prayers by types and suggest certain practices and patterns of prayer, remember that all of this are *aids* to prayer. They are a means to an end. As you work through this book and practice your prayers, remember that prayer is primarily about relationship, not about praying a certain way or using certain types and styles. One of my favorite stories is an old Jewish one which exemplifies this point.

> *There was once an illiterate cowherd who did not know how to pray, so instead, he would say to God: "Master of the Universe, you know that if you had cows, and you gave them to me to look after, I would do it for nothing, even though I take wages from everyone else. I would do it for you for nothing because I love you." A certain sage chanced upon the cowherd and heard him praying in this manner. The sage said to*

him, "You fool, you must not pray like that." The cowherd asked him how he should pray, and the sage set about teaching him the order of the prayers as they are found in the prayer book. After the sage went away the cowherd soon forgot what he had been taught and so he did not pray at all. He was afraid to say the usual prayer about God's cows because the sage had told him it was wrong to say such things, on the other hand he could not say what the sage had told him because it was all jumbled up in his mind. That night the sage was reprimanded in a dream and told that unless the cowherd returned to his spontaneous prayer great harm would befall the sage, for he had stolen something very precious away from God. On awakening the sage hurried back to the cowherd and asked him what he was praying. The cowherd told him that he was not praying anything since he had forgotten the prayers the sage had taught him, and he had been forbidden to tell God how he would look after his cows for nothing. The sage begged him to forget what he had told him and go back to his real prayers that he had said before ever he had met him.[2]

---

[2] David G. Gross and Esther R. Gross, *Jewish Wisdom: A Treasury of Proverbs, Maxims, Aphorisms, Wise Sayings, and Memorable Quotations* by (Fawcett Books, 1993).

Introduction

Prayer is different for each of us, just like the communication between any two people is different. Use the guidelines and examples in each chapter to find your own way, so that for you, like the cowherd, God will find something precious in your prayer life—not because you follow a set practice you found in this book, but because you have found a way of prayer that helps you express your prayers, not someone else's. Your prayer life will be based on what you have learned, what you have heard, and what you have been told, but you should take that and made it your own. Give it back to God as a gift. If that means, for you, telling God you will look after his cows for free while you stand dirty and unkempt in a field, so be it. God is pleased.

Studying the Bible

The Bible was written thousands of years ago, over a period of about 1,200 years, in a culture that is not like ours. That gap sometimes means that we will need to explore the ancient context to avoid misunderstandings. While we might wish that "God's Word" would not need such study, it is just not so (though I do believe that the major things God wants us to know are clear). God chose to direct his Word through humans, who are fallible and limited. God also chose to have these documents *preserved* by humans. The Bible did not drop down from heaven with its words divorced from a particular time, culture, or historical setting. If God had chosen to make everything easy for a 21st century Christian to understand, then an ancient person would have found much of it baffling. It is easier for a modern person to figure out how ancient people thought and viewed the world than the other way around. So God, in His infinite wisdom, chose for the Bible to be preserved in the Ancient Near East and the Greco-Roman world, in Hebrew, Aramaic, and Greek, and with all the historical and cultural peculiarities that go along with those contexts. Sometimes we will have to do some digging to make sure we understand a passage.

But there is more. It does not take a lot of detailed study to realize that each book of the Bible has its own style and character. God did not quash the personalities and styles of the writers He chose—He allowed them to write in their own way. This should not surprise us, for God has always worked through people without making them into robots or automatons.

If we wish to understand these ancient texts, we must try to bridge the gap between that world and ours. That means learning some of the history, culture, language, and society. This may be the hardest part of studying the Bible. Even today, people who travel from the Western world to the Middle East find themselves confused (and even offended) by that culture (and the reverse is true, too). The Bible portrays a Middle Eastern culture two or three thousand years ago, and that span of time adds even more differences. The good news is that many researchers have spent centuries studying those cultures, and their work is available. In this book, it is my task to sort through it all and bring the most important elements to you, to help us all enrich our prayer lives.

Once we have contextualized a passage, there is an important question to ask about what a prayer passage teaches us. Is there a *practice* that God commands, or is it a *principle* couched in ancient cultural language? For example, some New Testament passages urge women to keep silent in public gatherings (e.g., 1 Tim 2), while others depict women speaking freely in public worship (e.g., 1 Cor 11). Some might dismiss this as an example of the Bible contradicting itself, but that is a simple and narrow view of cultures, history, and life. Just like today, there were subcultures in every part of the Empire. Just like today, there were differing situations and contexts even within a subculture. There were places in the Roman Empire where it was considered inappropriate for women to speak in public in some circumstances; there were others where it was acceptable. So one possible interpretation is that these passages reflect different subcultures and not a particular practice we must follow. Instead, there a *principle* we should follow: "people ought to act appropriately in public assemblies." What they should or should not do depends on the culture and time. However, we could adopt a different interpretation and say, no, Timothy was writing a practice for us to follow, and God does not want women speaking in public. Paul (in 1 Corinthians) ignored that issue because he was addressing a much deeper issue about disorderliness in worship. Which one makes more sense to you? Can you think of other options? This example shows the importance of studying the Bible with humility and an awareness that we may not have all the answers.

Let's look at another example. It was the practice of the earliest Christians to meet in homes, and the New Testament implies that this is what Christians should do. Is this a practice commanded by God in a literal sense: "Christians should meet (only) in homes"? If so, many of us have violated the word of God by building church buildings for worship. Or maybe the issue is a command that "Christians should meet regularly." *Where* they met was a matter of culture, history, and necessity.

All this should lead us to realize that we must also critique ourselves. We tend to argue that something we are *already* practicing is a broad principle rather than a literal command; the rest of the passage is cultural. Or, if we practice something as a literal command, then we think that it is clear that scripture teaches it as such! In other words, it is easy to search and read Scripture to support what we already believe and practice.

What if what we "think is obvious" is incorrect? Take a look at the passage in 1 Peter 1.3–4, which commands women not to braid their hair or wear jewelry. Most of us would suggest that command was cultural. Yet could we be guilty of imposing our culture on Scripture? It is a difficult question. Sometimes, studies that contextualize can help. For example, there is good reason to think the passage was initially addressing a particular situation. In some areas of the Roman Empire, prostitutes braided their hair and wore it loose, while most married women wore hair bound up. Some Christian women, especially Greek women, may have thought that "being free in Christ" meant being free some social restraints. Perhaps the writer of the letter wanted to ensure that Christian women did not appear to be like immoral women. Another option could be this: since the Roman Empire drew strict divisions between classes and status, perhaps the writer did not think worship was a place to divide by class (which would be obvious by the clothing and adornment one wore). With these two pieces of information about the Roman Empire, we can reasonably conclude (without choosing between them) that the issue was larger than just how women dressed—there was a principle at stake rather than a specific practice.

It is not always so simple, of course, and sometimes we just do not know enough to make complete sense of a passage. However, such ambiguous passages are rare, and rarely impact a core theological or doctrinal practice. (It is also important to note that our salvation does not depend on the proper interpretation of every practice. God offers grace—not only for our sins against Him and others but also for our fair misunderstandings about church practice.)

In this study of prayers, the same questions arise. Asking those questions and studying the contexts, can tell us a lot about how to understand a prayer. I use a common, three-part method of study and interpretation. While not able to answer all questions, it usually helps reveal some cultural practices that can alert us to a possible misreading or misunderstanding. This three-part approach seeks to look "behind the text," "in the text," and "in front of the text."

Behind the text. Every story or passage of scripture has an original context. It took place at a particular time, in a particular place, within a particular social and culture setting. Knowing as much as possible about those contexts provides some sense of the meaning and purpose of a passage. That, in turn, gives us some guidelines as to what the passage could mean (or could not mean). There was an original audience for whom the text was written. For example, Paul wrote First Corinthians to the church that was located in the city of Corinth, to deal with problems and questions they had. Knowing more about ancient Corinth at that time helps us understand the letter.

In the text. Scripture is written communication, that is, it is literature. The writers chose certain phrases, words, and styles to communicate God's message. They used literary devices, such as symbolism, parallelism, or chiasmus. Just like we might in an English literature class, we can analyze those elements for better understanding. Often, a story that begins and ends with a similar phrase or event tells us something important about what is the middle of the story. Furthermore, these stories were not usually written down until long after the event. How did the *later* writer's history, culture, and purpose affect how the story was told? There are levels to the literary context.

In front of the text. This is often the most difficult approach because *we* are in front of the text. We must critique ourselves and our preconceived notions. Just as the ancient writers had a cultural and social context, so do we. As you and I read a passage of the Bible, we have our biases, expectations, and worldview that we bring to the text. In other words, we read the text through the lenses of our culture, personality, and experiences. How might that cause us to misread or misunderstand a passage? The more aware we are of our own context, the better we can avoid reading a passage in a way that might blind us to its original meaning or purpose.[1]

Pulling together all three of these methods gives us a better reading of the Bible. At a minimum, we are being responsible with our reading. When we take the context of God's word seriously, we honor it for what it is, as opposed to just reading it for what *I* think it mans, as if the only meaning it has is what I give it. Even if this approach does not give us answers, it can make us aware of problem areas, so we will not be too dogmatic and judgmental of a different understanding. Almost always, though, these methods make the passage come alive and the message clear.

Once we have finished the three-part approach, and have a decent understanding of the prayer and its context,

---

[1] If you want to read more about these methods, see my short book, *Let the Bible Speak: A Simple, Three-Part Method for Bible Study*.

we ask ourselves "what does this prayer teach me?" How can you use it in your world, your context, and your life?

This approach reveals the richness of the prayer passages in the Bible, which, in turn, serves the purpose of this book: to enrich our prayer lives.

The Types of Prayers

In this book, I divide prayers into nine types (or categories). By "type" I mean the content and the purpose of the prayer. The types, as I define them, are the following:

1. Praise
2. Thanksgiving
3. Petitions
4. Intercessions
5. Prayers of Confession and Repentance
6. Laments
7. Prayer-Vows
8. Blessings
9. Curses

Some of these types will be found together in one prayer, but more often than not (and perhaps surprisingly) most prayers are of one type. Some occur more frequently than others. The Psalms contain every type—not surprising since the Psalms is a book of prayer-hymns.

Most of us tend to use only a few of these types, the most common being petition, intercession, and thanksgiving. Studying *all* of the types, and learning their purpose and how to use them, will help us have a more consistent, rich, engaging, and effective prayer life.

Each type has its unique value and purpose so that we will examine each one on its own. We should not forget, however, that these kinds of prayers are connected and can be combined. For example, in the book of Exodus, some types repeat in a clear pattern. Suffering (slavery) leads the Israelites to offer a *petition*; the petition leads to an answer from God (choosing Moses as a leader), but also brings further difficulties (the Egyptians make the Israelites suffer). The sufferings cause the Israelites to offer more *petitions*, *intercessions*, and *vows*, and that results in God delivering the Israelites from the Egyptians. The deliverance leads the people to offer prayers of *praise* and *thanksgiving*.

As we study each prayer type, remember that the flow of the prayers is important, too. If we petition God for deliverance and then neglect to praise or thank Him, we have missed part of the rich connectedness of prayer types. God desires a relationship that does not place us in the role of a child who takes without thanks, nor that of a spouse who always cries out for help but never shows gratitude. It is a relationship that ebbs and flows, gives and takes, cries and comforts, declares and responds.

Prayers of Praise

A "prayer of praise" is a prayer that focuses on the character of God. It is not a prayer that thanks God for something, although thanksgiving prayers and prayers of

The Types of Prayers

praise are connected. Some might suggest this is too fine a distinction, but there is value in considering the two types as separate, even if they often overlap in practice. Consider this: while a thanksgiving prayer offers thanks to God for something He has done, a prayer of praise honors God because of who He is as Creator, the One who sustains us, and the One who loves us with perfection. Praise is about the recognition of God's being and character, rather than thanking Him for something he did.

Think of a famous person from history, someone you respect and admire above others. Let's leave Jesus out of this exercise—think of a regular human. Maybe it is a president, a king, a sports figure, a scientist, or an artist. You might, at first, be more in awe of who they are, rather than being thankful for something they did. The respect or awe that you feel is because of their character and being—their legacy, so to speak. The awe you experience is similar to the reason for a prayer of praise.

It may be difficult for us to offer pure prayers of praise. Most of us are pretty good at thanksgiving—we receive something good from someone, we thank the person. But the Bible contains plenty of models of praise-prayers for us to study and mimic. The opening chapters of Revelation provide a good example. Chapters 2 and 3 depict a pretty sad scene among the churches in Asia minor. They are poor, they have forgotten their way, pagan culture has influenced them, or they are selfish. A faithful Christian might feel quite disheartened. Chapter 4 is a scene that takes place in heaven. God is on His throne, surrounded by twenty-four elders and all manner of creatures; all are praising God. In such a dismal state of affairs on earth and in the church, they praise God because they know that He is *always* on the throne, He is always in control, He is *always* sovereign. We offer prayers of praise to God because He is in His holy temple; because He has the Final Word. We offer prayers of praise because *we* know how this story ends, regardless of how bad everything might be now.

When my children were young, we visited many of the ancient church cathedrals in Europe. My daughter, who was seven years old, did not like going inside those massive edifices. My wife and I thought that it was because of the crypts and grave markers inside. My mother had recently died, so we assumed the reminders of death made her think of her beloved grandmother. Once, on a trip to France, we visited the famous cathedral in Strasbourg, and I decided to have a serious conversation with her about her fears. As we walked down the center aisle towards the massive transept, I held her hand and asked why she was so scared of cathedrals. She stopped and leaned into me, looked up with wide eyes and said, "Because they make me feel *so* small. It scares me. I feel *this* big—" and she held out a thumb and forefinger close together.

I knelt down put my arms around her. "Yes, they *do* make us feel quite small, don't they?" I said. "But you know what? They built them that way *on purpose*. They designed them to be so big and to seem to reach to heaven, to help us remember how powerful and *awe*-some *God* is. And yet, despite all that scary power, we can still come to Him, and be with Him, just like we can be in this cathedral: because He loves us."

A look of wonder came into her eyes and she cocked her head to the side. "Really?" From that moment, she

The Types of Prayers

enjoyed visiting cathedrals. She lit candles for her grandmother in their chapels and touched the foot St. Peter's statue in Rome. She came to understand that the feeling of *smallness* was appropriate before God, for it reminds us of His power and His love.

That is why we offer prayers of praise.

Thanksgiving Prayers

Thanksgivings occur throughout Scripture. The basic words for "thanksgiving" appear 140 times in the Old Testament and 53 times in the New Testament. Paul's letters are full of thanksgiving prayers. Jesus gives thanks for people, for the fact that God hears him, and before meals. In the Revelation to John, elders, multitudes, and beasts offer thanksgiving to God twenty-four hours a day. In each of those instances, they thank God for something He has done for them—as an individual or as a group. Sometimes, though, thanksgivings are offered when they seem to make no sense. For example, the prophet Habakkuk stands on the walls of his city and sees disaster coming as an enemy bears down on Israel.[1] Yet he says, "Even so, I shall exult in the Lord and give thanks to the God of my salvation." (Note the combination of praise and thanksgiving in his prayer.) He praises him for who God is, then he thanks him because He is the God of his salvation.

---

[1] Habakkuk 3.16–17.

Sometimes, thanksgiving prayers are inappropriate. For example, Jesus tells a parable of a religious leader who goes up to the Temple to pray. He sees a tax collector—people who worked for the Roman oppressors and got rich off their own people—and he thanks God that he is not like him or other "undesirables." Jesus criticizes this sort of thanksgiving.

Thanksgivings are structured in many ways; they can be long or short, they can be spontaneous or well-planned. For this study, I define a thanksgiving as a prayer which thanks God for something specific that He has done—usually for the one who is praying, or for his or her community. It can also be a thanksgiving for what God did for someone else, following after requests by the one offering the prayer. In that case, the person thanks God for answering a petition was offered for someone else.

As with all prayers, thanksgivings are relational. They are part of the give-and-take of an ongoing conversation with God. Just like human relationships, thanksgivings can include understanding and misunderstanding, conversation and silence, joy and pain. Thankfulness is part of any genuine relationship, but it is not all of it. Thanksgiving prayers do not stand alone. They are connected with the prayers that came before: petition, vows, confession, repentance, and requests for forgiveness. In this case, a thanksgiving prayer is the response of gratitude. Still, we might offer a thanksgiving prayer merely *because* God allows us to have a relationship with Him, much like we might say "thanks for loving me" to a spouse or friend. It also means that we can offer a thanksgiving in the midst of struggles, like Habakkuk, just as we might say, "thank you for being here and comforting me" to a friend who visits us. Thanksgivings might be the most connected of all the prayer types because of the variety of situations in which it can be offered. While a petition, vow, or confession are usually offered in particular occasions, a thanksgiving prayer is always appropriate. This is why Paul tells the Thessalonian church to "give thanks in all circumstances; for this is the will of God in Christ Jesus for you."

Petitions and Intercessions

Petitions and intercessions are both common in Scripture. Both share the characteristic of asking God for something: they are both requests made of Him.

A petition is a prayer that asks for something for the one who is praying. It is a personal request. "God, please help me be generous today" is a petition. It might seem selfish to ask things for ourselves, yet it is part of a genuine relationship. Children ask their parents for things, and it is a sign of reliance. Of course, over-reliance becomes a sign of selfishness. Someone who is always asking for something does not experience a genuine richness of a relationship. But in connection with other types of prayer, petition is an appropriate part of the give and take.

An intercession, or intercessory prayer, is one which asks for something for someone else. I might pray that my wife has a good day. You might pray that a friend has successful heart surgery. We might pray that a missionary group is safe and effective. Praying on behalf of someone reflects that, as believers, our relationships are both vertical and horizontal. We pray *to* God the Father as our sustainer and redeemer, we pray *for* someone else as a loved one, fellow believer, or fellow human.

Both types of prayers are frequently found in scripture, though not as frequently as prayers of praise. We might find this surprising because most of us tend to ask for things far more often than we offer praise, thanks, confession, or repentance. This may be why we are sometimes dissatisfied with our prayers: we are missing the richness of a genuine relationship because we focus on only one or two types of prayer.

Why does Scripture suggest that prayers of intercession and petition should not be the most common types offered? The answer is, as noted above, that we need a relationship with God. But there is more to it than that. God first desired a relationship *with us*. He created us, He continues to create us, and He makes it possible for us to know Him. If petition and intercession stand alone, we turn God into a divine Santa Claus or a personal counselor. Scripture does not portray God in such a way. Instead, He is described as a father, mother, savior, creator, king, nurturer, and sustainer. Therefore, petitions and intercessions are only *part* of an ongoing relationship. If we use them alone, they are an insult to God and the relationship. Imagine if your child, spouse, sibling, or friends never thanked you, praised you, or said they were sorry. What if, most of the time, they only asked you to give them things? It would not be much of a relationship. In fact, it is not a genuine relationship at all.

Petitions and intercessions show our dependence on God and are appropriate within a full relationship. Because we praise, thanks, confess, and vow—we can also ask.

The Types of Prayers

Confessions and Prayers of Repentance

Confession and prayers of repentance, like the other types, are actions that are part of a genuine relationship. In fact, confessing and repenting may be the most intimate form of communication. There would be no need for confession and repentance if we did not fail our created purpose and damage our relationships with God and others.

Confession is not something we are prone to do. We do not want to confess our misdeeds; we want to explain them. We might say: "I was afraid" or "he provoked me beyond my limits." Those excuses might be true. But confession and repentance do not address the *reason* behind a sin; they speak to the *fact* of sin and the consequential damage.

Confession and repentance are about admitting our misdeeds and pledging to do better. "I am sorry I hurt you, and I promise I will never do/say that again." We often want to add "but..." to an apology. However, true confession rejects explanation or rationalization. If we try to offer defenses and reasons, we soil the process. Instead, confession should be a declaration; repentance is a pledge to be better.

Confession and repentance are linked, but they are different. Confession is the first part: I declare my sin before God, my spouse, family, friends, and/or congregation. When we name the sin, it begins to lose its power over us. Turn on the light, and shadows become common and ordinary. "It is not a goblin's head; it is my basketball!" "It is not a gnarled old man with a knife; it is the way the shadow of a tree shines against the curtains!"

When we move our sin from *inside* of us to *outside* of us, we begin to allow God to deal with it appropriately. Likewise, once it is out, it is harder to put it back (that is, to continue it). Once you have told someone of your sin, it is more difficult to ignore or rationalize it. You are held accountable—and accountability is crucial for the connected prayer type of repentance.

Repentance comes from an old Anglo-Norman/Old French word meaning "to renounce (something)," "to cease (to do something)," "to express contrition or regret." After confessing, we express our regret for the damage or hurt we have caused, and reject that behavior. A prayer of repentance disavows the act. "That is not who I am; it is not who I should be, and I reject it; I am now on a new path to avoid it in the future because I see it for what it is." A prayer of confession without repentance, or repentance without confession, would be incomplete.

The Bible is full of confessions and prayers of repentance. In much of the Old Testament, they are connected with sin sacrifices. Leviticus and Numbers both describe how they are to be offered to be cleansed of sin and forgiven. [2] These actions of sacrifice emphasize that one must confess sins to be forgiven for them. Jesus emphasizes the same thing in the Lord's Prayer.[3] During the conquest of Canaan, when the people failed to follow God's commands, tragedy fell upon them. Joshua went

---

[2] See, for instance, Lev 5.5; 16.21; 26.40; Num 5.7.
[3] See Matt 6.12.

The Types of Prayers

to the leader of the rebellious group and told him he must confess to God.[4]

Sometimes leaders confess the sins of a group of people to God, even though it may be that the leader himself did not sin. Ezra confessed the sins of his people for not separating themselves from nonbelievers, as God had asked them to do.[5] Nehemiah offers similar prayers for his people.[6] In Nehemiah 9.3, the people themselves confess their sins together as a group. Today, congregations and groups of believers rarely engage in public and group confession, despite the numerous examples in the Bible. This is probably a testament to the difficulty of admitting we are wrong. While some of us might confess in private at times, or (more rarely) in public, rarely do we hear leaders take on the sin of their congregation or a group and confess on their behalf as their leader.

If you do not know how to pray a confession, the Psalms are a good resource. Often, the words can be recited with little or no change to fit your circumstances. For example, Psalm 38.18 is an excellent beginning for a prayer of confession:

> *I confess my iniquity;*
> *I am sorry for my sin.*

It is a simple declaration of confession followed by a simple statement of repentance. A more complex prayer

---

[4] Josh 7.19.
[5] Ezra 9-10.
[6] Ezra 9-10.

is David's prayer of confession after his affair with Bathsheba.[7] The structure of the confession is a good template for our prayers:

1. Request for mercy (51.1–2)

2. Confession of the sin (51.3)

3. An acknowledgment that the sin hurts God and others and God would be justified in punishing (51.4–5)

4. An expression of knowledge that only God can forgive and cleanse (51.6–12)

5. A look to the future (repentance) (51.13–18)

6. A statement of knowledge that God wants sincere and humble followers (51.18–19).

When we sin, we can always be forgiven and start anew—otherwise, our sins would continue to build up, burying us under the weight of failure and guilt and separating us from God. This was the reason for daily, monthly, and yearly sacrifices described and commanded in the Old Testament. For Christians, there is no need to offer those oil, grain, or animal sacrifices, because of the sacrifice of His Son, made by God, took the place of those sacrifices. That perfect sacrifice was more horrific than any animal sacrifice, but also more effective

---

[7] Ps 51; read the story in 2 Samuel 11-12.

The Types of Prayers

because it was God's sacrifice.[8] It need be done only once. Then, in confession and repentance, we take part in that sacrifice. Jesus becomes *our* offering for *our* sins of his own free will, and we are cleansed and forgiven.

In prayers of confession and repentance, we throw ourselves upon God's mercy, acknowledging that He is our only hope to begin again. We make a statement about our future, and we commit to being renewed, to live differently, and to serve Him. Such prayers offer us the opportunity to offer ourselves in humility and to be lifted up by the Judge himself, who says, "go, my child; you are no longer guilty. The sacrifice of sin has been paid. You are a forgiven and sinless being—now go out and live like it."

Prayers of Lament

A lament is a prayer that cries out to God in pain and loss. It does not ask God for anything (though a petition often follows a lament). Imagine a small child who is in pain and cannot fathom what is happening to them. The child cries out to their parent because the parent is the caregiver, the authority, and the nurturer. The child may even wonder why the parent is allowing the pain, though

---

[8] People are often outraged that the Jewish religion slaughtered thousands of animals a year for their own sins, but often those same people are not outraged that a man was slaughtered for their sin. We should be shamed that it was necessary, and grateful that it was offered.

the parent may be unable to stop it—perhaps it is an illness, or an inoculation, or a cut on the arm.

For that reason, offering a lament may be the most open of prayers, because laments are an emotional cry. Laments in the Bible sometimes even question God, or call Him to account! In a time of seemingly meaningless suffering, a lament may come to the lips of a believer almost unbidden: "why, God?!"

You may have heard that one should never question, criticize, or be angry at God. This ignores the richness of prayers of lament we find in the Bible. A lament is God's way of allowing us to be honest with Him and express, with pure emotion, how we feel. Like confession and repentance, lament is deeply relational. After all, if a relationship forbids certain discussions, then it is a limited relationship. There is nothing improper about a lament, because one is *still* turning to God, like a child crying out to a parent. For this reason, laments often end with petitions, and sometimes with thanksgivings or praises. This does not mean that God always makes clear the reasons for the suffering. Yet those who pray laments in the Bible find comfort in the presence of God, even if relief does not come, just like a baby finds comfort in its mother's arms, even if the pain does not go away.

There are a few laments in the early books of the Old Testament. Hagar cries out when she and her son are banished to the desert to die.[9] Joshua and the leaders of Israel lament when they inexplicably lose a devastating

---

[9] Gen 21.16. See "Hagar's Lament and Petition (Gen 21.16)."

The Types of Prayers

battle.[10] Laments are found most often in the Psalms and in the Prophets,[11] especially those written during the time of Exile.[12] The New Testament is not without laments, though they are rare because of the number of letters or epistles rather than stories. One of the most famous is from Jesus, while on the cross, quoting a Psalm of lament (Ps 22):

> *My God, my God, why have you forsaken me?*
>
> *Why are you so far from helping me, from the words of my groaning?*
>
> *O my God, I cry by day, but you do not answer; and by night, but find no rest.*
>
> *Yet you are holy, enthroned on the praises of Israel.*
>
> *In you our ancestors trusted; they trusted, and you delivered them.*
>
> *To you they cried, and were saved;*

---

[10] Joshua 7.7–9. See "A Lament (Joshua 7.7–9)."

[11]

[12] For example, see Psalms 17:13–14; 35:4–6, 26; 44; 58:7–10; 137 (more than 20% of the Psalms are laments). The entire book of Lamentations is a highly developed lament-prayer.

> *in you they trusted, and were not put to shame.*
>
> *Jesus uttered other laments as well over two cities and Jerusalem.[13]*

The Psalms include both individual laments and community laments: a lament can be offered by a congregation or other group of believers in a time of tragedy, suffering, and loss. A lament is a good example of the relational nature of prayer and is a type that can add some meaningful richness to our prayer life.

Prayer-Vows

Prayer-vows, like laments, are relatively uncommon today, at least in the modern Western world. Yet they are prevalent in scripture. Perhaps this is a form of prayer that we should revive as a way to add richness to our prayers. You can judge for yourself after you have studied some them later in this book.

Vows offered to a deity were quite common in the ancient world among all people and religions. A prayer-vow is a conditional agreement with a god or goddess. The offerer promised to give a sacrifice or a gift of some sort, in return for the god or goddess doing something for them. For example, in 296 BC, the Roman consul Appius

---

[13] Matthew 11:20–23 (cf. Luke 10:13ff); Matt 23:37–38 (Luke 13.34–35).

The Types of Prayers

Claudius Caecus prayed that, if his patron goddess Bellona would give him victory in battle, he would build a temple in her name.[14]

The Old and New Testament both contain prayer-vows of a similar nature. Sometimes the offerer promises something to God and asks nothing in return. For example, a Nazarite vow is one in which a person promises not to cut the hair, drink wine, or be around unclean things for thirty days.[15] John the Baptizer took this vow, as did Paul.[16] Samson is one of the most well-known examples of a man taking a Nazarite vow, though this vow was for his entire life rather than just thirty days. These one-sided vows, where God is not asked for anything, are vows of dedication—dedicating oneself to God in some particular way for a particular time.

The second type of vows are conditional agreements with God, and are common in the Bible, too. The offeror promises to give something to God, or His work in the world, if He grants their petition. For example, Hannah vows that if God allows her to give birth to a son, she will dedicate him to the service of God.[17]

Since these vows are pledges to do something *if* God does something in the future, we might wonder if they are self-serving. While a prayer-vow could be misused

---

[14] Ovid, *Fasti*, vi.201–205. The Temple was built several years later in Rome, and dedicated on June 3, 296 BC.

[15] The full description and requirements of the vow is found in Number 6.1–21.

[16] Luke 1.15; Act 18.18, respectively.

[17] 1 Samuel 1.11–17.

in that way, a genuine prayer-vow is part of the relationship between God and us. It is a give-and-take, a promise to each another, and a way of showing loyalty. We are not telling God that he *must* do something; just that if He does, we will thank Him by offering a special gift in place of a usual thanksgiving. It might be money, time, or some other benefit to God and His mission.

Two-sided vows are serious business. Psalm 66 cautions that, if you dare to offer such a vow, you had better keep it. One should think carefully and responsibly *before* offering a prayer-vow. Jephthah offered one rashly in Judges 11, with tragic results when he found out his vow meant he had to do something he had not foreseen.[18] Vows of this type should be treated with care.

The one-sided prayer-vow is an opportunity for us to show our dedication to God and a way for us to hold ourselves accountable to Him. We might vow to pray three times a day for the next month, or refrain from critical words for a day, or to skip lunch for a week and spend that time in study and prayer.

---

[18] Some question whether he should have kept the vow, since it involved the sacrifice of his daughter; or whether this was an example of Israel's fall from God in offering human sacrifices. We will examine his vow in the next volume, "Rash Vows (Judg 11.30-31)." (There is a later writing that describes the daughter's long lament: Pseudo-Philo, *Liber Antiquitatem Biblicarum* 40.5–7. If you are interested in a technical discussion of the prayer, see my analysis in Markus McDowell, *Prayers of Jewish Women: Studies of Patterns of Prayer in the Second Temple Period*, 100–104.)

The summarize, a prayer-vow is a type of prayer that is used to hold ourselves accountable to God, dedicate ourselves to God, and expand our possibilities of prayer.

Blessings and Curses

Blessings and curses appear in Scripture as separate prayers but usually appear together. The reason for this is because they are a particular kind of petition. They do not ask God for something as much as wish it or hope for it, usually in the presence of another person or in public.

A blessing asks that good will come upon someone, that they will receive a gift, or that seeks the best for them. Curses do the opposite: they ask that punishment or harm may come upon someone. In this way, they are petitions that God do something, though they often do not ask God directly for the blessing. For example, Naomi says to her daughter-in-law, "May you be blessed by the LORD, my daughter" (Ruth 3.10).[19] Noah says, "Cursed be Canaan, the lowest slaves shall he be to his brothers" (Gen 9.25).[20] There is an element of "hope" rather than a direct request.

I use the word "hope," yet prayer-blessings and prayer-curses are stronger than a mere "I hope this happens." In the ancient world, blessings and curses (especially the

---

[19] See Ruth 3.10, which will be addressed in the next volume of this series, *Praying Through the Bible: Volume 2 (Judges–2 Samuel)*.

[20] See "Noah's Blessings and Curses (Gen 9.25-27)."

latter) were thought to have an almost magical power. If one said them correctly, in the right circumstances, they would happen. The understanding of curses and blessings in the Old and New Testament is rarely, if ever, presented in that "magical sense." Still, they have more power than just "I hope God brings justice upon you." Prayer-blessings and prayer-curses attest to a strong belief in the spoken word and the ear of God.

Blessings are pronounced upon individuals, groups, or nations. Leaders and priests utter them; ordinary people speak them. Blessings can be pronounced upon God (and often are). In the latter, the blessing almost becomes a kind of praise/thanksgiving/blessing; that good should come to God because He deserves it.

Non-believers in the Bible sometimes offer blessings. Melchizedek blessed Abram (Gen 14.19-20); [21] King Hiram blessed Solomon (1 Kings 5.7); the Queen of Sheba blessed the God of Israel (1 Kings 10.6). Blessings can be for something specific or merely a general pronouncement of good. They can be formal or informal, spontaneous or traditional.

Jacob (Israel) blesses his grandsons in a traditional "deathbed" pronouncement upon children (Gen 48.15-20). [22] The priest Levi blessed all the people of Israel (Lev 9.22). [23] The book of Ruth is filled with prayer-blessings upon a number of people. In the New Testament, Elizabeth blesses Mary (Luke 1.42, 45); Jesus

---

[21] See "Melchizedek Blesses Abram (Gen 14.19-20)."
[22] See "Israel blesses the Sons of Joseph (Gen 48.15-16, 20)."
[23] See "Aaron Blessing the People (Lev 9.22)."

The Types of Prayers

blesses children (Mark 10:16) [24] and offers blessings at meals (Luke 9.16). Paul's letters are filled with teaching about blessings, blessings on God, and blessings on his readers. [25]

Curses, likewise, can be general or specific, formal or spontaneous. In scripture, they are usually the result of some evil done by a person or a warning of what will come if someone does something forbidden. Joshua curses anyone who might try to rebuild Jericho (Josh 6.26);[26] Jeremiah curses the day of his birth and the person who announced it (Jer 20.14–18). We might think the New Testament would be sparse with curses, but there are plenty. Peter offers a curse when he denies that he is one of Jesus' followers (Mark 14.71);[27] Paul pronounces a curse on anyone who preaches a different gospel than the one he taught (Gal 1.9).

As noted, blessings and curses often appear together, in a formula style: "if *this* then a blessing, if *that* then a curse." Noah blesses two of his sons but pronounces a curse on the third because of his shameful actions against his father (Gen 9.25–27).[28] Jesus offers four blessings and then contrasts it with four curses or "woes" (Luke 6:20–26). The book of Revelation contains many blessings and curses—a whole series of them are found in Revelation 22.7–18.

---

[24] See the parallels in Matt 19.15 and Luke 18.17.
[25] See, for example, Romans 12.14; 1 or 7.40; 2 Cor 1.3; Eph 1.3.
[26] See "A Curse-Prayer (Joshua 6.26)."
[27] He does it twice in Matthew 26.72, 74.
[28] See "Noah's Blessings and Curses (Gen 9.25-27)."

These examples of prayer-blessings and prayer-curses show us that they can enrich our prayer lives. It is likely that most of us do not think too deeply about blessings, only offering them before meals, weddings, and other particular occasions. Yet blessings can play a larger role in our lives, as we will see in this book. Curses are more difficult—many of us might think that God would not want us to curse anyone. Curses can be misused: Rebekah places a curse on herself to help her son deceive his father (Gen 27.12–13).[29] Abner pronounced a self-serving curse (2 Sam 3.9). In the New Testament, Paul wrote: "bless and do not curse" (Rom 12.14). But he is writing only to those who are persecuting his readers. How can curses be used correctly in a modern Christian life?

The best way is to learn about them in context. We will read a few of them in this book, and you can decide for yourself the most responsible way to use them.

---

[29] See "A Blessing Wrought in Deception (Gen 27.7, 12–13, 27–29; 28.2-4)."

Genesis

Introduction

Genesis means "beginning," and that is what this book describes: the beginning of the world and the beginning of the people of Israel. The first four chapters are like an epic, with no set time or place. There is a lot to learn about who God is, why he created humans, and what the relationship is between people and God. Beginning with chapter 12, we learn about the origins of Israel, its early history, and its special relationship with God.

The first thing that might strike you about the prayers in Genesis is how much variety there is among them. All sorts of people offer them—from kings to prisoners—in all kinds of situations: birth, death, joy, and suffering. Some of the prayers are long and formal. Some are only one sentence. The prayers offer rich models for us to draw from for our own prayers.

There are fourteen prayers: five blessings, five petitions, two intercessions, two vows, and one each of a thanksgiving, a lament, and a curse. The context encompasses everything from the birth of children to prayers for the whole nation of Israel. Some of the prayers are used for deceptive purposes. One is offered by a pagan priest!

The variety of prayer in this first book show that prayer can take on many forms and styles, contexts, purposes, and situations. These fourteen prayers serve as excellent beginning in our journey to develop a richness in our own prayer lives.

The Personal Name of God (Gen 4.26)

At that time people began to invoke the name of the LORD.

Background

Ancient people believed that there were many gods. They differed in personality, characteristics, abilities, jurisdiction, and power. For instance, *Ba'al* was the Canaanite god of rain and storms. He did good by bringing rain for the crops, but he could also wreak havoc through floods and storms. When there was a drought, *Ba'al* was thought to have been imprisoned by another god. To the Egyptians, Re was the sun god and Hapi was the god of the Nile River. When God performed miracles on the Nile River (see Exodus 7–8), the Egyptians saw this as a defeat of Hapi by the God of the Hebrews. There were gods of fertility, gods of war, and gods of art and science. Gods of childbirth, gods of healing, and gods of each specific craft. Most were rarely heard from unless a human did something to get their attention (good or bad). On occasion, a god or goddess would become fond of a particular person and would bless and protect them.

Though it might seem strange those who practice Judaism, Christianity, or Islam, these gods did not care much about ethics or morals. They placed few, if any, demands on humans (other than to respect the gods). Humans existed to serve the gods when required.

God is entirely different. Genesis stresses that God created the world for humans, not for his own benefit. He nurtures people instead of seeing them as slaves. He cares how they live and how they treat each other. Ethical and moral behavior matter to this God.

In this passage in Genesis 4.26, we find the first mention of prayer in the Bible. It is not a long essay on the subject or even an example of prayer. It is a brief mention that, after the flood, people began to pray; that they began to "call on the name of the Lord." In the ancient world, to know someone's true name was to allow you into their life.

Meaning

It is not clear in an English translation, but the English word "Lord" used here is not a translation of the common Hebrew word *adonai*. The word means "lord," "sir," or "master." But here, the word is YHWH (or "Yahweh"), a strange word in Hebrew. It is probably a form of the Hebrew verb "to be," which is why many Bibles translate it as "I Am." A better translation, though more cumbersome, is "I will be what I will be." The word YHWH is not a general word of description, like *el* or *elohim* ("God"). It is not a title, like *el shaddai* ("God Almighty") or *el elyon* ("God Most High"). Instead, it is God's actual name. That name became so sacred to the

The Personal Name of God (Gen 4.26)

Jewish people that they later chose not speak it aloud. Instead, they substituted the word *adonai* or the phrase "The Name," or some other word or phrase.

In early Hebrew, only the consonants were written down (in order to save paper). In the seventh century AD, a group of Jewish scholars called the Masoretes decide to add written vowels to the consonants in the biblical text. When they came to the word YHWH, no one remembered the vowels, because the word had not been spoken aloud for centuries. So the Masoretes used the vowels from the word *adonai*, making up a word from part of both YHWH and *adonai*.[1] Those vowels and consonants are untranslatable and unspeakable by the rules of Hebrew grammar. So English Bibles usually use the word "Lord." To distinguish it from *adonai* (which is also translated "Lord"), most publishers print it in small caps ("LORD") and print *adonai* as a normal capitalized word ("Lord").[2]

In Exodus 6.2, Moses experienced the presence of God through a burning bush. When Moses asked who He was, God tells him that he is the one who appeared to Abraham, Isaac, and Jacob as *el shaddai* (a title). Then he tells Moses that he only made himself known to them in part, but now he is revealing his true name, YHWH, to Moses.

---

[1] Our English word "Jehovah" is an attempt at a transliteration of this mixed-up word: Y-H-W-H or J-H-V-H with A-d-O-n-A-I- or E-D-O-N-E.

[2] It is an interesting exercise to read through the first five books of the Bible, marking when each is used. If you wish to take on such a task, mark each with a different color as you read, and look at the pattern that results.

Yet we just came across the word YHWH here in Genesis, long before Exodus 6. How can that be? Well, the books of the Old Testament were passed down orally through many generations, eventually written down, and later edited more than once. It was the later editors who put the word YHWH in Genesis 4, probably because it is the first mention of God. The editor wanted to make it clear just who this God was: not some distant god, not some uncaring god, but the God YHWH himself, who had revealed himself to Moses at the burning bush. Remember, the people reading this story would already know about Moses and the burning bush. The name YHWH was so important that those who wrote down these stories wanted to make it clear from the first the character of this God.

Application

And what does it mean? It means He is the God who wants us to know Him in an intimate and personal way. He wants us to come to him, to share with him, and to be in fellowship with him. So he gave Moses, and us, his personal name to use when we "call upon" the Lord.

How do you usually address God in prayer? Is it formal? Is it familiar? Both are appropriate, for he is a powerful, terrifying presence who also wishes to be intimate with the people he created. The name YHWH captures this somewhat contradictory aspect of God—so sacred that Jews would not say it out loud, yet so intimate because it is his personal name. Spend some time in prayer to this God who cares about you so much that he is willing to make himself vulnerable to you. A God who is

The Personal Name of God (Gen 4.26)

prepared to run the risk of you hurting Him, rejecting Him, or ignoring Him. He was willing to risk all that, as God, in order to have the chance for an authentic and intimate relationship with you. How will you respond today in prayer?

Noah's Blessings and Curses (Gen 9.25-27)

"Cursed be Canaan;
lowest of slaves shall he be to his brothers."

He also said,
"Blessed by the LORD my God be Shem;
and let Canaan be his slave.

May God make space for Japheth,
and let him live in the tents of Shem;
and let Canaan be his slave."

Background

Most of the prayers in the Bible are one of four types: praise, thanksgiving, petition, or intercession. Yet the second prayer that appears in the Bible is one of the rare types: a curse and blessing.

Noah asked for a curse on his son Canaan, and blessings on his sons Shem and Japheth. Why? The previous events show that Canaan had acted with disrespect towards his father, while the other two protected and honored him. Showing disrespect for a parent was a great crime in the ancient world—some cultures punished it by death. Because Canaan broke this essential rule of ancient societies, he was condemned.

Most people pray for blessings, but rarely, if ever, pray for a "curse" upon someone.[1] Sermons or church classes about prayer almost never mention curse-prayers. Yet there are curse prayers in the Bible. What do we make of this genre?

God would not want me to ask Him to curse someone, would he? We might say that this was the Old Testament, before Jesus—now we love our enemies, we do not curse them (Luke 6.28). Paul echoes that thought in Romans 12.14. Revelation 22.3 implies that the curse pronounced upon humans in Genesis 3 will be reversed. They are found in New Testament as well. Matthew 25.41 is an example from the New Testament. Paul, in his letter to the Galatian Christians, is so angry with someone that he writes, "let that one be cursed!" In 1 Corinthians 16.22, Paul writes the same about anyone who does not have love for the Lord. Paul even wishes a curse on himself in Romans 9.3, if it would help his fellow Jews come to believe in the Messiah Jesus. Second Peter 2.14 pronounces a curse on those who engage in sinful behavior with full knowledge and intent. The warning at the end of the book of Revelation pronounces a curse on anyone who might add things to the prophecies contained in the book of Revelation.

---

[1] The technical term for a curse-prayer is an "imprecatory prayer."

Noah's Blessings and Curses (Gen 9.25-27)

Meaning

Curses are a part of the Bible and so a part of the communication between humans and God (though they are more rare than other types of prayer). If they should be a part of our prayer life, how should we use them?

It is a matter of perspective and responsibility. Even though we often find blessings and curses together, there are many more blessing-prayers in the Bible than curse-prayers. Jesus, on the cross, asked God to forgive his torturers, rather than to curse them. We should take extreme care before praying a curse. Curse-prayers are not divine grenades that I can lob at those who hurt me. God is not my personal hit man to do my bidding.

The best way to view curse-prayers is as a negative counterpart to prayers of forgiveness. God has forgiven me; I should forgive others. Jesus implies this concept in the Lord's Prayer in Matthew 6.9–13, then states it again in Matthew 6.14–15. If I desire forgiveness, I must extend it to others first. Before I ask God to curse someone, I should examine myself. Curse-prayers should not often be uttered. God is a God of mercy. Besides, we would want mercy from those who might want to curse us! Most of the curse-prayers in the Bible are aimed at those who intentionally, consistently, and even gleefully try to destroy God's work or God's people, or for those who attempt to twist the Gospel so that it destroys the message and hurts people. (The latter is the reason for Paul's emphatic curse in Galatians.)

Having a curse-prayer in your arsenal is like having a drop of potent poison in your possession; it has the power to hurt others and to hurt you. Maybe it is best if we never offer one, or reserve it for the most devastating and far-reaching circumstances, as in scripture. I would suggest that we not use curse-prayers at all until we have finished a good portion of this journey through the prayers of the Bible. Then, perhaps, we will have a context to understand the proper use of curse-prayers (and we still may never wish or need to pray a curse).

On the other hand, blessings are easy to understand. In contrast to curses, blessings are a healing balm that should be sprinkled liberally on all. To understand the context of the blessing and curse-prayer in the current passage, read the paragraph just before the prayer (Gen 9.20-24). Because Canaan dishonored his father in public during a vulnerable moment, Noah utters a curse-prayer on Canaan's descendants. Shem and Japheth, however, are blessed, for not only did they refuse to participate in Canaan's sin, but they covered their father, without looking, thus treating him with honor. They showed proper respect to their father and deserved blessings because of it.

Application

Who can you ask God to bless today? Be specific, just as Noah is specific in this prayer, both in the person and the kinds of blessings you want God to bestow on the recipient. Be generous, as God is generous.

Melchizedek Blesses Abram (Gen 14.19-20)

*"Blessed be Abram by the God Most High,
The One who created the heavens and the earth.
And blessed by the God Most High,
Who delivered your enemies into your hand."*

Background

We might assume that the Bible only contains prayers by Jews or Christians. Yet there are prayers in the Bible by people who are neither. We might then think that these must be prayers to their pagan gods, and sometimes this is true. One example is in the book of Jonah where a group of sailors pray to their gods to deliver them from a storm. But there are also instances of pagans offering prayers to the God of Israel. Today's passage is one of those. Melchizedek, a priest-king of the Canaanite god El, offers a prayer of blessing for Abram.

This is the third prayer in the Bible and is the second blessing. Abram, a man chosen by God, has his nephew taken captive during a battle. When Abram hears of the capture, he gathers his forces and rescues his nephew. On his way back home, he passes by a town known as Salem (the city that would later become Jerusalem). Melchizedek comes out to meet Abram and his entourage. Though Salem is a pagan city at this time, and although Melchizedek is the High Priest to the pagan god El, he offers a blessing upon Abram, which Abram accepts.

Meaning

Does God hear the prayers of pagans? How can this story enhance our understanding of the practice of prayer?

Melchizedek is a mystery. Who was he? Why does Psalms 11.4 and Hebrews 7.1-7 speak of him as if he were a Hebrew priest? The Bible is not the only ancient writing that presents Melchizedek as important figure. The Dead Sea Scrolls, written and preserved by a conservative Jewish sect in the time before Jesus, also wrote of Melchizedek as an important person. He appears to be doing the work of God in spite of his role as a pagan priest. Maybe it is because of the importance of Salem/Jerusalem. It is the place, by tradition, where Abram almost offered his son Isaac in sacrifice (Gen 22). Jerusalem would later become the political and religious center of Israel. It is the Holy City. Maybe this story foreshadows the things to come. Or maybe it is a way of showing that this location has always been special to God, even when it was a pagan city. That is, God was present in (Jeru)Salem centuries before it became an Israelite city during the time of David.[1]

It is not unusual for God to use mysterious, unknown, or unusual people—even pagans—to bless his people (as well as punish them). Cyrus of Persia, the pagan king of that country, is even described as the "anointed one" (messiah!) of God in Isaiah 53-55, because God used him to return the Jews to their land after the exile (see the books of Ezra and Nehemiah). The passages in Isaiah about Cyrus was later read as a prophecy about the coming Messiah Jesus by the New Testament writers.

Melchizedek blessed Abram in the name of God—or did he? When we look at the words of the blessing itself, we find that there are four lines, two of which refer to "the Most High God." That phrase is a translation of the Hebrew phrase *el elyon* which we encountered in Genesis 4.26,[2] which was the first mention of prayer in the Bible. The title *el elyon* is not found often outside the Bible, but the title *el* was used by Canaanites to refer to their supreme god, the god who created people. Melchizedek might be praying that his own god bless Abram. But the use of *el elyon* might lead us to think that he was asking Abram's own God to bless him. Or maybe the writer of Genesis just wants us to know that God heard the prayer, regardless of Melchizedek's intention.

This prayer has a simple poetic structure: A-B-A-B. The "A" sections address God as "the Most High," and the "B" sections give a description of God as creator.

---

[1] See 2 Sam 5.6–10.
[2] See "The Personal Name of God (Gen 4.26)."

Note that even though this is a prayer that asks for a blessing upon Abram, its main focus is on God—the One who gives blessings. Biblical prayers often focus on God even when the purpose of the prayer is to ask for something. In grammatical terms, we can say that God is the "subject" of the prayer; humans are the "object" of the prayer.

Application

Is there someone who has blessed you, even though they are an unbeliever? Maybe they did not say a specific blessing on you, as Melchizedek did for Abram, but perhaps God used that person to bring a blessing. Write the name of the person and what happened. Devise a prayer to thank God for that person, and the fact God used them as an instrument for your blessing.

You might also choose someone you know and write your own brief blessing-prayer, like Melchizedek's, using the A-B-A-B structure. Make God the focus of the prayer as you ask for a blessing for that person.

Abraham Intercedes for Abimelech
(Gen 20.7, 17)

Now then, return the man's wife; for he is a prophet, and he will pray for you and you shall live.

Then Abraham prayed to God; and God healed Abimelech, and also healed his wife and female slaves so that they bore children.

In our journey through the prayers of the Bible, we draw a distinction between the meaning of a "petition" and an "intercession." As noted in the Introduction, many people use the terms as synonyms, but we will emphasize subtle distinctions in the goal of enriching our prayers.

Background

This is the first instance of an "intercessory" prayer in the Bible, though they are common throughout. It is an intercession by Abraham on behalf of a man named

Abimelech and his family. The context teaches us a lot. Abraham and Sarah had entered a new land, and Abraham was worried that the men would kill him and take Sarah for themselves. Though Abraham showed great faith when did as God asked and left his home (Gen 12.1), others stories show his lack of faith. He did not trust God to fulfill the promise of a child, so he took matters into his own hands in the story in Gen 16. In fact, the current situation had happened before! In Genesis 12.12-13 Abraham was afraid local men would kill him and take his wife (Gen 12.12-13). Here, it is as if he had forgotten that God had protected him before. Abraham had still not learned his lesson.[1]

Abraham and Sarah are on a journey and are led by God to a place called Gerar. Abraham is afraid that someone will kill him and take his beautiful wife, so he tells the same story he told in Genesis 12: she is his cousin.[2] The King of the region, Abimelech, believing Sarah to be Abraham's sister, sends for Sarah to make her his wife. God then afflicts all the king's household

---

[1] Some scholars suggest that the stories are so similar, maybe they are two tellings of the same event, mixed up by later editors who were unaware it was the same story. I am not convinced that editors were any less observant than modern-day scholars. Maybe they included it twice to emphasize Abraham's lack of faith. While it is not possible to know for sure, we only need to look at our own lives to know that we also show the same lack of faith we have shown in the past, in spite of God's protection.

[2] This is not a complete falsehood, because she is his half-sister. However, it would have been more important to the inhabitants of the new land to know she was his wife!

Abraham Intercedes for Abimelech (Gen 20.7, 17)

so they cannot bear children. It might seem a little unfair of God to punish Abimelech for being misled by Abraham. Maybe this is part of the guilt that Abraham must bear: the consequences of his lack of faith and hiding the truth brings unfairness upon others.

But God does not leave it there. He gives a dream to Abimelech, warning him that Sarah is another man's wife and that he is about to die. Abimelech protests, in truth, that he did not know! God tells him to go back to Abraham and have Abraham offer a prayer on his behalf (an intercession). Abimelech does so. Abraham prays that Abimelech and his household will be healed.

Meaning

What can we learn about prayer from this story? God not only protects Abraham, but he warns King Abimelech that he will die unless he returns Sarah to Abraham. Furthermore, when Abraham prays for Abimelech and his household, God answers his prayer. In spite of Abraham's lie and his lack of faith in God's promise, God protects him, gets him out of the mess, and then answers his prayer! What an example of God's forgiveness and generosity. We learn that God hears our prayers even if we have not acted in faith or trust and have caused a mess of things.

Application

Think of times that you have lied or acted with dishonor to protect yourself. This story suggests that God will listen to your prayers regardless. Consider times you have trusted in yourself, not God, and hurt others as a consequence. God is still willing to protect you and hear your prayers. That is the message of this passage and this prayer: if we belong to God, he listens to us—even when we fail to hear to Him.

Make a few notes in your journal about people you have hurt through your own selfish or self-protective behavior. Then, spend some time in prayer offering intercessions on their behalf. Ask God to heal them, to save them, and to restore them from the trouble you have brought upon them through your actions. He will do it, for He is faithful—even when we are not.

Hagar's Lament and Petition (Gen 21.16)

And as she sat opposite him, she lifted up her voice and wept.

Have you ever cried while praying? I don't know of many who have (or admit it), but a lot of people in scripture do. Maybe it is a difference in cultures. People of the Ancient Near East tend to be more demonstrative than Westerners. Today's reading is the first instance of someone crying while praying, and it is also the first lament.

Background

The story of Hagar is a central story in the history of the Jews, and some of its results still echo today in tensions in the Middle East. The background to this prayer is that God promised Abraham and Sarah that they would have a child. Yet a lot of time had passed, and there was still no child. Sarah suggested that Abraham take her maidservant, Hagar, as a "surrogate mother." This was not a surprising suggestion at that time in history. A slave was property and could be required to do perform such a service. More important to understanding the story, a child did not "officially" become part of a family until a covenant ceremony took place (for the Jews this later became circumcision). Blood relation was less important than a covenant. So the child of Hagar would be the child of Abraham and Sarah in law and society.

Hagar complied and gave birth to a son, who called "Ishmael," which means "God hears" in Hebrew (an interesting choice considering that Abraham and Sarah made it happen on their own initiative). According to what we know of birth practices in the ancient world, Hagar sat on Sarah's lap as she reclined back and gave birth, emphasizing the symbolism that the child was Sarah's. This story is another example of Abraham's lack of faith in God's promises. He (and Sarah) seemed to believe that "God helps those who help themselves" (a phrase that appears nowhere in the Bible).

Not too long after the birth of Ishmael, Sarah becomes pregnant, just as God had promised. Ishmael became a useless and unwelcome appendage to the family: no long an heir, just a mere slave. But he was still the son of Abraham. Sarah did not like this, and perhaps saw him as a threat to her natural son's inheritance as the firstborn. We can imagine poor Hagar, who had only done as asked. Abraham succumbs to Sarah's complaints and sends Hagar and Ishmael away into the desert. They had used Hagar for their own purposes, being impatient with God. When God delivered on his promise, Hagar became more than useless: she was an irritant. It is unfair. It is unjust. Could we blame Hagar for being upset with Abraham and Sarah? Or even for being upset with God?

Hagar's Lament and Petition (Gen 21.16)

Instead, she sets her small son down, then walked a few hundred yards away. She did not want to see her son die. She cried to God. We do not know her words, but it not hard to guess. She was a faithful slave, did as she asked, and when circumstances changed she was sent to die with her child to make the situation easier on her masters. A situation of their own making. And God heard her.

This story has striking parallels to the story in Genesis 32 about Abraham's near-sacrifice of his natural son, Isaac. There, an angel tells Abraham that he must sacrifice his son to God. He and Isaac leave for the desert in the early morning (22.3), just as Abraham sends Hagar and Ishmael out into the desert in the early morning. In Genesis 32, an angel came to Abraham to stop him from sacrificing Isaac (32.11-12); Hagar cries to God, and an angel comes to her. In Genesis 32, an angel directs Abraham to a ram caught in a bush to take the place of Isaac as a sacrifice (22.13); the angel directs Hagar to some water, so she and her son will not die. Finally, the Hagar narrative is an example of Abraham's lack of faith; the Isaac story is an example of how he finally came to trust God completely, even to the point of sacrificing the promised son.

Meaning

This is yet another Genesis story depicting humans who rely on their own wants and desires instead of trusting God. And, as usual, things become a mess. Instead of waiting for God in His time, Abraham and Sarah took matters into their own hands, and the result was an unwanted mother and child in exile and near death. Once again, God comes to the rescue. Not only does He save Hagar and Ishmael, but he promises that Ishmael will also be blessed by God and have many descendants, just like Isaac. It was not God's original plan, but human sin required him to clean up the mess. He does so by granting great blessings.

Sometimes, while praying, we may feel like we don't have the right to cry out to God because we caused the problem. Or maybe someone else has caused the problem, but they have such power over us and the situation that we see no way out, like Hagar. This story shows that God still cares. He hears when we cry out in pain, and he comes along to do triage, to give first aid, and then to perform healing surgery.

Application

Write in your journal today about something you are suffering now, small or large, which came about because of human weakness and self-centeredness. Maybe, like Hagar, you tried to do the right thing, but other people and circumstances have resulted in your pain. Or maybe, like Abraham or Sarah, you are the cause of the suffering. Think about these things, then cry out to God about them, knowing that He hears and heals.

A Chain of Prayers
(Gen 24.12-14, 27, 42-44, 48, 52, 60)

"O LORD, God of my master Abraham, please grant me success today and show steadfast love to my master Abraham. I am standing here by the spring of water, and the daughters of the townspeople are coming out to draw water. Let the girl to whom I shall say, 'Please offer your jar that I may drink,' and who shall say, 'Drink, and I will water your camels'—let her be the one whom you have appointed for your servant Isaac. By this I shall know that you have shown steadfast love to my master."

"Blessed be the LORD, the God of my master Abraham, who has not forsaken his steadfast love and his faithfulness toward my master. As for me, the LORD has led me on the way to the house of my master's kin."

When Abraham's servant heard their words, he bowed himself to the ground before the LORD.

*"May you, our sister, become
thousands of myriads;
may your offspring gain possession
of the gates of their foes."*

Up to this point in our journey through the prayers of the Bible, we have encountered isolated prayers. A prayer appears in the midst of a story: a blessing, curse, petition, or intercession. It reflects how we offer most of our prayers: "let us now praise God" in church, "let's thank God for the food" before we eat dinner, and "let's pray for the sick among us."

Sometimes, however, our prayers are a series of prayers about the same subject, which might stretch out over hours, days, or maybe years. The passage for today is just such a series, or a chain, of prayers. It concerns a servant's search for a suitable wife for his master, and it demonstrates how many types of prayer can create a chain over time, flowing in and out of related events.

Background

Isaac needed a wife, and his father, Abraham, wanted him to marry someone from their own tribe rather than from the alien land where they lived. Abraham sends a servant on a journey back to the family's homeland. When he arrives, we can almost imagine him saying to himself, "now that I am here, how do I go about finding a wife for my master?" What does he do? He prays. He asks God for success in his mission. Notice how specific he is in this prayer: "Let the girl to whom I shall say, 'Please offer your jar that I may drink,' and who shall

A Chain of Prayers: Petition-Thanksgiving-Blessing (Gen 24.12-14, 27, 42-44, 48, 52, 60)

say, 'Drink, and I will water your camels'—let her be the one…"

We might be uncomfortable with that of a request to God. Perhaps it seems like we are manipulating Him. Or maybe we fear we might interpret some event as an answer from God when it is not. Those are worthy concerns, but they should not keep us from being specific when we speak to God. Say what you think. Tell Him what you want in detail. God will hear, and then do what he knows is best. It is then our task to listen with discernment and humility.

As soon as the servant makes his request, so it is. His reaction is instructive. He does not immediately jump about shouting, "Praise the Lord, He answered my prayer!" Instead, he is discerning and careful. He has faith, but it is not a blind faith. He doesn't want to read more into the situation than he should, nor does he wish to allow his desire to succeed affect how he interprets the events. In spite of his particular prayer, he understands human weaknesses. So he "waits on the Lord."

As the servant and the woman talk, he learns that she is from the clan of Abraham! She invites him back to her home, and the now servant believes that God has answered his prayer. He offers a thanksgiving (24.27), saying, "Blessed be the LORD, the God of my master Abraham, who has not forsaken his steadfast love and his faithfulness toward my master. As for me, the LORD has led me on the way to the house of my master's kin."

When they arrive at the family compound, the family listens to the servant's story and the purpose of his journey. He repeats the whole story (including the prayers in 42-44, 48). Having heard the story of his mission, Rebekah's family also believe that God is directing these events. They agree to give their daughter to their clansman in marriage. The servant offers another thanksgiving and a praise to God.

But the parents don't want to part with their beautiful daughter at that moment. The servant pleads with them: he has on a long journey already and it will take a long time to get back. His master is waiting. So the parents ask the daughter what she wishes, and she says she is ready to go. Her parents ask God for a blessing upon her and the marriage. "May you, our sister, become thousands of myriads; may your offspring gain possession of the gates of their foes."

Meaning

Note the flow of prayer throughout this story: petition, answer, thanksgiving. The servant tells the story, which includes the petition, answer, and thanksgiving. Then, a second petition and a thanksgiving. Finally, a blessing. Prayers in the Bible often have such a flow about them; one type of prayer leads to another. Confession to forgiveness to thanksgiving. Lament to petition to praise. And here, petition to thanksgiving to blessing.

Application

Try your hand at writing a prayer with each of the following types: petition, intercession, thanksgiving, praise, lament, forgiveness, repentance, curse, and blessing. Draw arrows to depict some of the flow patterns you

A Chain of Prayers: Petition-Thanksgiving-Blessing (Gen 24.12-14, 27, 42-44, 48, 52, 60)

might make a chain of these prayers. Consider some situations in your life that might fit one of those patterns. Spend some time in prayer, trying out these chains of prayer.

Finally, consider your current situation and your prayers. Could you be at the beginning of a pattern? In the midst? Maybe you have a need today: start with a petition. Or maybe you need to repent: start with a confession or a prayer of repentance. What will come next? Leave some blank pages in this part of your journal, and make a note to come back to it. Keep track of the flow of prayers for the situation.

Intercession and Petition for a Child
(Gen 25.21, 22)

Isaac prayed to the LORD for his wife, because she was barren...

If it is to be this way, why do I live?" So she went to inquire of the LORD.

For most people, having children is a desire and a goal. This has been true throughout history and in all cultures. For many, the inability to have children causes great disappointment and even shame. The importance of having children may come from the fact that we are made in the image of God: because He is creative, we desire to create, too. The miracles of conception, gestation, and birth are the work of God, but the fact that two humans can come together, become "one flesh" and create new being is an ultimate creative act for people. Likewise, the birth of a child gives a parent someone to love and to care for, just as God created us to have someone to care for and love. We have created a "family," we have someone to carry on the family name, and we find fulfillment through nurturing, teaching, and protecting another human life. In the Old Testament, the concept of "life after death" is not found until the later books. The early stories imply that eternal life was sought through one's children.

It is true that some people are called to be single, or choose it, and through that they fulfill a different role in the world (1Cor 7.1-7, especially verse 7). Paul wrote that singleness is a gift. Some will not be able to give birth, yet they can adopt the unwanted, or serve others by helping children. The important function of "being fruitful and multiplying" is fulfilled in many ways other than having children, though that may be the primary way (Gen 1.28, 9.1).

Background

In the ancient world, having children was perhaps more important than today, since they viewed having children as the only way to gain "immortality." Note the number of stories in the Bible which contain the theme of the "barren woman" praying for a child.[1]

Just as Abraham and Sarah did not conceive for a long time, so also their son Isaac and his wife Rebekah could not conceive. Instead of trying the alternative method of his parents, Isaac turned to prayer: he "prayed for his wife." Though he is shamed and disappointed by their

---

[1] Sarai (Gen 11); Rebekah (Gen 25); Rachel (Gen 29); Samson's mother (Judges 13); Elizabeth (Luke 7); as well as general references to barrenness (Exod 23.36; 1 Sam 2.5; Ps 113.9; Luke 23.39). There are also a number of passages that use "barrenness of the womb" as an analogy for barrenness of land, people, or spirituality.

Intercession and Petition for a Child (Gen 25.21, 22)

lack of success, he seems more concerned for her. He interceded for her, God answered his prayer, and Rebekah becomes pregnant with twins.

As her pregnancy progressed, the twins within her womb were quite active. They were "struggling with each other." Like her husband, she turns to prayer. She petitions God for an answer to all this activity. God answers her, just has he answered Isaac. The struggling in the womb is a prophetic act, a foreshadowing of the future. The descendants of these two boys will comprise two great nations who will struggle against each other. We know that this is what happened: the nations of Israel and Edom had many conflicts through the years.

Meaning

Like many couples, my wife and I experienced a time when we were unable to conceive the children we wanted so much. We did what many couples do: we sought the advice of doctors, we tried various medical and popular remedies. But, using Isaac and Rebekah as models, we also turned to prayer. It was challenging and disappointing for us because God stayed silent for four long years. Then, he blessed us with a wonderful son. Four years later, without any delay, the blessing of an equally wonderful daughter came to us.

During those first four years, we knew that God's answer might be "no." Maybe, for whatever reasons, God thought it best that we not have children. Or maybe our pain was happening because we live in a fallen world, and that can result in difficulties, and, for whatever reason, God chooses not to remedy it. Maybe his answer was "you need to adopt, because I have children who need parents," or "you need to live childless because I need some childless parents for my work." Those would have been difficult answers for us to hear. Yet we still knew that the first step was intercession and petition, and waiting on the Lord.

In retrospect, it is easy to see how our focus on prayer got us through that time. In the midst of it, we did not always feel faithful. We doubted. We wondered about God. At times we were angry. But in the midst of difficulties, God does not require that we *feel* the right way. Only that we do what faith requires. Throughout the Bible, believers question God, show anger with God, and show frustration with Him. But they do not give up talking to Him. This is a crucial lesson for the practice of prayer.

Application

Think of something in your life or the life of someone you know. Is there something you (or they) desire, but do not seem to attain? It does not have to be giving birth. Many other significant things are part of being human. Maybe you are not married but wish to be. Maybe someone is dying and you wish they would not. Write it down in your journal, then offer intercessions and/or petitions for it. Remind yourself that it is okay to be frustrated with God—even angry. But keep talking to Him. Like Isaac and Rebekah, learn to speak your concerns to God. And, like Isaac and Rebekah, allow Him to answer as He will. It is an opportunity to practice the virtue of patience as you "wait on the Lord."

A Blessing Wrought in Deception
(Gen 27.7, 12–13, 27–29; 28.2-4)

Bring me game, and prepare for me savory food to eat, that I may bless you before the LORD before I die.'

I shall seem to be mocking him, and bring a curse on myself and not a blessing." His mother said to him, "Let your curse be on me, my son; only obey my word, and go, get them for me."

So he came near and kissed him; and he smelled the smell of his garments, and blessed him, and said,
"Ah, the smell of my son
is like the smell of a field that the LORD has blessed.
May God give you of the dew of heaven,
and of the fatness of the earth,
and plenty of grain and wine.
Let peoples serve you,
and nations bow down to you.

Be lord over your brothers,
and may your mother's sons bow down to
you.
Cursed be everyone who curses you,
and blessed be everyone who blesses you!"

May God Almighty bless you and make you
fruitful and numerous, that you may become
a company of peoples. May he give to you
the blessing of Abraham, to you and to your
offspring with you, so that you may take
possession of the land where you now live
as an alien—land that God gave to Abra-
ham.

Background

These prayers are another set of chain-prayers: prayers that are connected and repeated as part of the same event. This passage one of the more troubling stories in Genesis—both the story itself and the questions it raises about God. A mother (Rebekah) helps her youngest son (Jacob) deceive her old, blind husband (Isaac) to gain the blessing that belonged to the first-born son (Esau). When the father discovers the deception, he tells the older son that there is little he can do. When the older son threatens the younger, the younger runs away. Not only does God allow this to happen, but He also accepts the ill-gotten blessing as valid. The prayer-blessing is a key element in this story: it is repeated or referred to twenty-

A Blessing Wrought in Deception (Gen 27.7, 12–13, 27–29; 28.2-4)

three times in the space of fifty-two verses![1] There is also a curse connected with it in three other places (27.12, 13, 29).

In the ancient world, the oldest son inherited the status, position, and half the wealth of his father. Upon the death of the father, the household would become his and his own sibling become subservient to him. The official blessing of the father on the eldest son was a sacred event, often coming near the time of death. The blessing solemnized the transfer, much like a marriage ceremony or the covenant birth ceremony in a previous prayer passage.[2]

Yet this story is more complicated than just a mother playing favorites. Long before the deception takes place, Esau gave away his inheritance to his brother Joseph for some food. Was that a valid transfer of birthright? Did Rebekah know of it? Some suggest that the problem is all Esau's fault: he was so cavalier with his inheritance, he *deserved* to have it taken from him. But if that is true, and the transfer was binding, then why was the deceit necessary? Esau may be at fault, but Rebekah and Jacob are not worthy characters in this story.

Even God's response is troubling. Though He judged others for their wrong actions within a family (Cain and Abel, for instance), here he treats Jacob as the heir in spite of his deceptions. The younger receives a blessing; the older receives a curse! Why does God condone this

---

[1] Gen 27.4, 7, 10, 12, 19, 23, 25, 27, 29, 30, 31, 33, 34, 35, 36, 38, 41; 28.1, 3, 4, 5, 6.
[2] See "Intercession and Petition for a Child (Gen 25.21, 22)."

behavior? The prophet Malachi will later write that "God loved Jacob, but hated Esau." Paul quotes this passage in Romans 9.13. How are we to understand such a prayer of blessing that seems so unfair?

First, the quote about "hating and loving" comes from a prophet, the words of which can rarely be read literally. In the book of Malachi, "Jacob" stands for the nation of Israel and "Esau" stands for the nation of Edom. Edom had been devastated, and Israel was trying to rebuild their city after their return from Exile. People were questioning God. Why do some do well and others not? Saying, "God loved Jacob but hated Esau" is a poetic and symbolic way of saying, "some of the ways of God are a mystery."

Still, we wonder. Did God want *Jacob to be the patriarch rather than Esau? If so, why? He was not the older son. Did God just make the best of what happened after it was over? Jacob is not an admirable character until much later in his life. He bargains with God (e.g., Gen 28.20-22), deceives his father-in-law (30.37-43, 31.20), and more.*

Meaning

In our prayer lives, we should learn to embrace mystery. God does some things; He does not do others. He in control, He will do what He knows to be best, and sometimes His reasons or purposes will lie beyond our understanding. We are called to believe and trust—not to understand everything—because He is God. We do not always have to make sense of His actions; we only have to follow.

A Blessing Wrought in Deception (Gen 27.7, 12–13, 27–29; 28.2-4)

That is one lesson about prayer that we can take from this story. But there is another. God does not reject us because we sin. We might even deceive our spouse or father, but He does not reject us. What matters is that we stay in relationship with God and keep trying. This is the second thing we can learn about prayer from this story. In prayer, we can—and should—*struggle* with these kinds of issues. We should wrestle with God. That may sound strange, but note this: God later changes Jacob's name to "Israel" (*yisra-el*), which means, "one-who-struggles-with-God" (Gen 32.28). Jacob struggled with God physically, mentally, emotionally, and spiritually. He was not always noble, and he was not always right. He was in a relationship with God, fighting and wrestling to find his place. He never gave up on God, and God never gave up on him.

We often rationalize our actions, just as Jacob did. "He *sold* the inheritance to me!" We all tell white lies (at least!), and bend the truth for selfish gain. The hopeful message of the blessings in the story is this: even if we do such things, God's plan will *still* be fulfilled. We do not thwart the plans of God. If we allow Him in our lives and never stop wrestling with Him, He can pick up the pieces of *our* mess and bring healing and change. And bless us when we don't deserve it.

Application

Think of someone you believe does not deserve a blessing. Perhaps it is you. Write the name down in your journal and ask for a blessing upon that person, because that is what God does: blesses us even though we don't deserve it. You might use the two blessings in this story as a starting point for your prayer. First, ask that the person be wealthy and well fed. Then, request that they have plenty of help, to be honored and blessed by others, for their enemies to be stopped, for their children to be healthy, and for them to live happily in the land.

Jacob's Vow
(Gen 28.20-22)

If God will be with me, and will keep me in this way that I go, and will give me bread to eat and clothing to wear, so that I come again to my father's house in peace, then the LORD shall be my God, and this stone, which I have set up for a pillar, shall be God's house; and of all that you give me I will surely give one tenth to you.

In modern world (at least in the Western world) we do not offer many prayer vows. Many may not even know what a "prayer-vow" sounds like. Yet, there are fifteen passages that include prayer vows.

Background

A vow is a special kind of prayer wherein the offerer makes a promise to do something. Rather than asking for something, thanking God for something, praising Him, or offering a confession, it says, "God, I will do *this* for you." Prayer-vows do not only occur in ancient Judaism.

Babylonians, Canaanites, Greeks, and Romans all offered prayer-vows. These usually asked a god or goddess for some benefit, and then pledged to do something in return, such as offering a sacrifice or giving money to a temple. There are several prayer-vows in Homer's *Iliad* by Greek men pledging to Athena if she will give them victory in battle.[1] The Roman Claudius Appius raised his hands to heaven and prayed, "Bellona, grant me the victory this day, and a temple shall be yours."[2] Often, an offering was made in conjunction with the vow (called "votive" offerings).

Vows in the Old Testament are similar to these in form and function, though sometimes nothing is asked of God. A vow is a statement of intention. For example, a Nazarite vow is a special vow that one makes to refrain from cutting one's hair, drinking wine, or being around unclean things for thirty days.[3] Some of the prayer-vows seem positive and constructive; others seem selfish. For example, in 1 Samuel 1, Hannah makes a vow that if God will give her a son, she will dedicate him to God.[4] That child becomes the great prophet and leader of Israel, Samuel. Yet the vow that Jephthah makes before a battle turns out to be a terrible mistake, because he made a rash promise to sacrifice the first thing that greeted him

---

[1] For some examples, see Homer, *Iliad* 6.86–101, 305–10; 10.284–94.

[2] Livy 10.19.17.

[3] See Numbers 6. Paul mentions the Nazarite vow in Acts 21.23-26.

[4] See 1 Sam 1 .11–13, 15, 17.

Jacob's Vow (Gen 28.20-22)

upon his return home. That "first thing" turned out to be his daughter.[5]

There are firm commands in the Bible, that, if you offer a vow, you better keep it (Ps 66.13-20; Malachi 1.14). We should take care not to be rash or secular in our own vow-making.

Here, Jacob's vow occurs near the beginning of a long narrative about him. All through his story, until the end, Jacob is selfish and deceitful. In the vow he offers, it *does* sound as if he is trying to manipulate God. He is worried about his safety, and he prays, "if you'll be with me and bless me, I will take you as my God." Notice that the vow comes second—first he asks God to be with him. This is backwards: "you can be my God if you'll give me something for it." It is an improper prayer-vow.

Yet God blesses him anyway, and it is later clear that he blesses him *in spite* of the vow, not because of it. It was God's plan all along. However, at the end of the story Jacob *does* keep the vow. The place where he made the vow later became a famous sanctuary known as Bethel ("house of God").

---

[5] The explanation for this is found in the arrangement of homes. Most were compounds with fences around them which held the animals—especially prize animals. He probably thought it would be an animal he would first meet, and he was willing to sacrifice it, even if it was his best specimen. Yet it was Jephthah's daughter who greets him (see Judges 11.30-31).

Meaning

Some of us might think that making such a prayer-vow sounds like "making a deal" with God, and we have been told that bargaining with God is improper. This probably comes from stories such as the one about Jephthah, or because we should not "put God to the test."[6] But the Bible contains more positive examples of vows than negative. The emphasis is often on the actions of the one making the vow. If your primary purpose of a vow is to get something you want, it may be improper. The instructions about Nazarite vows and Hannah's vow for a son are good examples. Another is Nehemiah's call to the Jews to keep their marriages within their own people (Neh 13.25): he asks them to make a vow to God but does not suggest they ask anything in return. A prayer-vow stands as a symbol of the offerer's dedication to Him. Any response we request in return is just like a petition: He may grant it or not.

Application

What kind of vow could you make to God? It does not have to be something noble or difficult. Maybe you vow to pray five times today. Or you could adopt one of the vows we find in Scripture. For instance, the Nazarite

---

[6] See Deut 6.16; Matt 4.7.

Jacob's Vow (Gen 28.20-22)

vow lasts thirty days: refrain from drinking alcohol, cutting your hair (and shaving!), and do not go near dead bodies during that time. The purpose is to focus on the holiness of life and your dedication to God. If you are married, you and your spouse could vow to forego sexual activity for a period of time to focus on prayer instead.[7] The practice of self-denial during Lent is intended to help one focus on the meaning of the cross and the sacrifice of Jesus. All are appropriate, biblical ways of practicing the discipline of the prayer-vow.

Write in your journal about your experience in praying a vow and your ability to keep it. Note what the experience was like, and how it felt. Re-introducing the spiritual practice of a prayer-vow is an excellent way to enrich your prayer life and to renew your dedication to God.

---

[7] Paul implies that this is a practice for some Christians in 1 Cor 7.5.

Waiting in Prayer
(Gen 30.17-22)

And God heeded Leah, and she conceived and bore Jacob a fifth son.

Then God remembered Rachel, and God heeded her and opened her womb...and she named him Joseph, saying, "May the LORD add to me another son!"

Background

Today's devotional commentary is a story that I call "The Baby Contest." It is the story of Jacob's two wives, Leah and Rachel, and their desire to have children. As we discussed above,[1] the ability to bear children was important in the ancient world. Having a child—especially an heir—was an honor and a blessing. Having a child gave a woman status and brought honor to her marriage and family. In that world, being childless brought shame

---

[1] See "Intercession and petition for a child (Gen 25.21, 22)."

upon a woman. Many passages in the Bible address the "barren woman."[2]

In this story—which is intended to be humorous—Rachel and Leah vie for that honor by trying to out-do one another in the baby-making department. Yet the story is not in the Bible for mere entertainment; it also emphasizes how God blessed Jacob—abundantly!—and kept His promise. God told Abraham and Isaac that their descendants would be as numerous as grains of sand or as stars in the sky. Jacob finds this promise fulfilled in his own home.

The words of the prayers offered by Rachel and Leah are not included, but verses 17 and 22 show that both women offered petitions to God for children. Notice that this story has another instance of a slave acting as a surrogate mother, just as we read in the story of Abraham and Sarah.[3] This time, none of the dire consequences occur. The use of the slave here was not because of a lack of trust in God, but just of a desire to have children, and God blessed the family through that ancient practice.

Meaning

One of the lessons we can draw from this story is that God cares about the things we care about. He is concerned about our personal needs and desires. It mattered

---

[2] For example, see Gen. 11; 25; Judges 13; Psalm 113.9; Is 15.1; Luke 1.7, 36; 23.29; Heb 11.11.

[3] See "Hagar's Lament and Petition (Gen 21.16)."

Waiting in Prayer (Gen 30.17-22)

to Him that Leah and Rachel were shamed because they could not bear children for Joseph, so He granted their requests. While God might not always answer our prayers, or He might not answer as we wish, He does answer. (As the saying goes, "Sometimes He answers 'no'"). After trying for some time, Rachel does not become pregnant, so she turns to a surrogate, and God blesses her and Jacob through that slave. Later, "God remembered Rachel" (a biblical way of saying God decided to act on Rachel's prayer) and she becomes pregnant. Leah did not have the problem of barrenness that her sister did, but she did bear the stigma of being the "second choice" of her husband (see Gen 29). Many stories in the Bible depict God as a "champion of the underdog." Maybe that is why God blessed Leah with children and made Rachel wait. Leah was shamed by being the "second choice" even though she was the first-born daughter, so God granted her the honor of being the first to bear an heir.

Note how both women respond in prayer. Leah was the second choice of Jacob, yet she is happy to be blessed with children. Rachel was the first choice of Jacob, who is barren at first, but she is thankful to have a child (even from a surrogate). Both focus on the *blessings* rather than the difficulties. Both praise God for those blessings (verses 18, 20, 23, 24).

Notice the words the women use when they discuss *how* God answered their prayers. He "heeded," "gave," "endowed," and "remembered." God is a God who listens, understands, and remembers us and our pain. For some time, Rachel probably felt that God had forgotten her. But she "waited on the Lord" and He remembered her. Patience in prayer is something we can strive for, too.

Application

Look back through your prayer journal and note the responses to petitions that you have offered. Write a brief thanksgiving in the margin of each. Maybe God hasn't answered some (or any) of those prayers yet. In that case, write "I wait on the Lord" in the margin of those petitions. You might make a note of times you felt God had forgotten you, too—that is part of the "give and take" of prayer, as we see in Rachel's story.

What have you learned about "waiting" in this study of prayer? Make some notes about it, and then offer a new petition, taking into account what you have learned about waiting for God, about God remembering, and about how God's blessings come or do not come.

Jacob's Petition for Safety (Gen 32.9-12)

"O God of my father Abraham and God of my father Isaac,

"O LORD who said to me, 'Return to your country and to your kindred, and I will do you good,' I am not worthy of the least of all the steadfast love and all the faithfulness that you have shown to your servant, for with only my staff I crossed this Jordan; and now I have become two companies.

"Deliver me, please, from the hand of my brother, from the hand of Esau, for I am afraid of him; he may come and kill us all, the mothers with the children.

"Yet you have said, 'I will surely do you good, and make your offspring as the sand of the sea, which cannot be counted because of their number.'"

Background

This is another prayer by Jacob. This one also takes place in the wilderness, like the prayer-vow he offered in Genesis 28.20-22.[1] Jacob offered that prayer after deceiving his father into giving him the blessing intended for his older brother. This prayer acts as a frame, or a "bookend," with that prayer. The first prayer was offered when he was leaving home; this one is offered as he heads back home. He had left with nothing except the fraudulent blessing; he returns with two wives, many children, and fabulous wealth. God blessed him beyond measure. Despite the entourage of family and servants, Jacob is afraid, and for a good reason.

This prayer, and the attitude behind it, is quite different from the prayer-vow he offered when he left home. In that prayer, there was some arrogance, self-centeredness, and immaturity. He prayed that if God would protect him, he would adopt God as his own. Much has happened since that shallow prayer, and Joseph has matured. He spent many years working for Laban to win the hand of Rachel, only to be tricked into marrying the older sister, Leah, first. (Note how the "trickster" Jacob has been tricked himself, and that trick involved the rights of an older sibling, just like Jacob's trick again Esau.)

Jacob's prayer demonstrates that has matured in faith and integrity. As he approaches home, he does not known Esau's intentions. Is he still angry with him for stealing his birthright? Will he try to kill Joseph and his

---

[1] See "Jacob's Vow (Gen 28.20-22)."

Jacob's Petition for Safety (Gen 32.9-12)

family? Instead of trying to come up with a scheme or manipulate God, Jacob throws himself on the mercy and protection of God. He shows genuine humility and regret for his past deception. He begins by addressing God with majesty: "God of my father Abraham and God of my father Isaac,"—a prayer-opening that would become a standard for his descendants. Jacob then recalls all the things that God has done for him, and notes that he is aware he is not worthy. Contrast that attitude with his prayer-vow in Genesis 28.20-22.[2] Finally, he arrives at the purpose of the prayer: a petition for deliverance in the midst of fear and the face of the unknown. The prayer closes with an affirmation of God's faithfulness. It is a prayer that acknowledges God as sovereign, recognizes Jacob's own selfish past, and pleads with God to help him as the only One who can.

Meaning

This is the first example in the Bible of a formal, structured, petitionary prayer. It begins with an address and invocation, followed by a statement of the character of God, the petition itself, and then a final declaration of God's character or promise. We will read many similar prayers as we continue praying through the Bible.

Two elements of this prayer are helpful in our journey to enrich our own prayers. First, the structure described above is a good model:

---

[2] "Jacob's Vow (Gen 28.20-22)."

1. Address/invocation (calling on God with a title or titles due him)
2. Statement of what God has done in the past (perhaps how God has helped or answered the you in some other event)
3. Petition (be specific)
4. A statement of the faithfulness of God (he is a God you can trust because he keeps his promise)

Second, this prayer teaches us that our prayer life is a journey. We begin in immaturity and ignorance. We cannot expect to be fully mature in our prayers, and we should not be too hard on ourselves when our prayers seem simplistic. Paul notes that we often do not know how to pray.[3] God does not ask for perfection—he asks us to do our best. We do not have to *be* the best; we just have to be faithful.

Application

Write down the sections of this formal prayer in your journal. Use the structure to pray a petition. You may even wish to write down your prayer. You can refer to it later when you want to use this pattern for petitionary prayers.

---

[3] Romans 8.26.

Jacob's Petition for Safety (Gen 32.9-12)

Think about the journey of your prayer life. Where are you now? The beginning, the middle, or the end? Have you been praying long enough to look back and to how you have matured and learned? If so, write something about that; if not, then look ahead. Where would you like to be in six months or a year? Write down some goals, and check back on them once in a while.

Israel's Prayer for His Son's Success
(Gen 43.14)

"...may God Almighty grant you mercy before the man..."

Throughout this study, we have seen a recurring theme. Humans sin, find themselves in a predicament and cry out to God for deliverance. In spite of their disobedience, God answers their prayers and saves them.

Background

We see that pattern in this prayer, too, at the end of the long narrative about Joseph and his brothers. It is a story of jealousy, favoritism, betrayal, false imprisonment, and false accusations. Having read through to the end, we can see that God's hand was present the whole time. He used weak and selfish humans by turning their weakness to His purposes, and by answering their prayers through His blessings.

Growing up in the household of his father, Jacob/Israel, Joseph did not endear himself to his brothers. He acted arrogantly. His father played favorites with him to the jealousy of the other sons. After years of treatment as second-class siblings to the youngest, they sold him into slavery and deceived their father by telling him that a wild animal had killed Joseph. Yet, with God's help, Joseph rose up through the ranks in Egypt from a slave to the Pharaoh's right-hand man. When a severe drought covered the region, Egypt had already prepared for it because God helped Joseph interpret the Pharaoh's dream about that impending drought. So Jacob/Israel sends Joseph's brothers—except for the youngest, Benjamin—to Egypt for food, unaware that Joseph is not only alive but in charge of distributing food. The brothers come before him, but do not recognize him. Joseph knows them but does not reveal himself at first. He sets them up as if they had stolen from the Pharaoh. When their "crime" is discovered, Joseph imprisons one of them and demands that the brothers bring the father's youngest son as proof they are not spies. The brothers return to their father, but he refuses: he lost a favorite son once before; he will not risk losing another.

The famine becomes severe. The brothers know that they cannot go back to Egypt for food without Benjamin, if they do not go, they will starve. No longer immature and jealous siblings, they vow with their lives to keep Benjamin safe. The oldest, Judah, even promises the life of his own sons if anything happens to Benjamin. This is a different Judah than the one who sold Joseph into slavery.

Finally, Jacob/Israel agrees. His words reflect a sad resignation: he must risk losing another son, or the whole family will die. (Note the "savior theme" of a father who risks his special son for so that everyone else can live). Having made his decision, Jacob/Israel offers a brief

Israel's Prayer for His Son's Success (Gen 43.14)

prayer of blessing upon the sons. He asks God (*el shaddai*) to grant that the harsh Egyptian man will be merciful. It is all that he can ask: he has one dead son (so he believes), one son in prison, and the rest are off to an uncertain meeting in Egypt. He may lose them all. So he merely asks God for mercy. He tells the sons, "If I am bereaved of my children, so I will be bereaved." Jacob/Israel has given up on everything—except God. God will either save them or He won't. So be it.

Meaning

Have you, or someone you known, ever been in such circumstances? When all seems lost, when all that is left is to give it into God's hands, whatever may come. Chances are you *will* face that situation some point in your life. God allows tragedy, for his own mysterious reasons, and sometimes we are required to do what frightens us to our core. At first, we might argue, bargain, and deny. After a time, when our energy and emotion are sapped, all that is left is to say, is Jacob/Israel says: "So be it … I am not in control … it is in God's hands."

Despite the desperation and despair we might feel, this is a good thing. How can being at the end of one's rope be positive? Because it forces us to finally recognize our inability to control life and destiny. It forces us to throw ourselves upon the mercy of our Creator. To say, simply, "May God have mercy."

Application

Think of something you have struggled with, fought against, or have suffered through. Perhaps you are struggling today. Maybe you have struggled with God's silence or experienced terrible suffering that God did not alleviate. Jacob/Israel was a great man of God, and we might hesitate to compare ourselves to him. But recall the whole of Jacob/Israel's life, and take comfort that God renamed him "Israel"—"one who struggles with God." The namesake of the people of Israel struggled with God, just like you and I do. Imitate Jacob/Israel, offer your struggles to God, resign yourself to the reality that He is in control, and ask for mercy.

When we do that, we become part a long line of great men and woman of God who stood in that same situation and prayed that same way.

Israel Blesses the Sons of Joseph
(Gen 48.15-16, 20)

*"The God before whom my ancestors Abraham and Isaac walked,
the God who has been my shepherd all my life to this day,
the angel who has redeemed me from all harm, bless the boys;
and in them let my name be perpetuated, and the name of my ancestors Abraham and Isaac;
and let them grow into a multitude on the earth."*

"By you Israel will invoke blessings, saying, 'God make you like Ephraim and like Manasseh.'"

Background

This prayer, a blessing, come at the climax of the Genesis story. Of the fourteen prayers in Genesis, five are blessings and five are petitions. How do your prayers of blessings and petitions compare? In the informal surveys I have done over a period of twenty-five years, most people offer petitions and intercessions most often. The second most common is the thanksgiving prayer. The other types of prayers are rare: praise-prayers, blessings, prayer-vows, and curses—if they even find their way into our prayer lives at all.

It was common in the ancient world for a dying father to call his sons to him and pronounce official blessings upon them. This primarily served to confer official status on the oldest son as the one who will take the place of the father. Here, Jacob/Israel sees the two sons of Joseph for the first time and wishes to bless them. Recall a similar blessing prayer in Genesis 27 and 28, which also involved Jacob/Israel himself. There, Jacob/Israel tricked his poor blind father into blessing him instead of Esau, the oldest son. Now it is Jacob/Israel who is an old, blind man offering a blessing on his grandchildren. Those grandchildren will become the Patriarchs and namesakes of two of the tribes of Israel. As he prepares to bless them, Jacob/Israel places the hand of honor (the right hand) on Ephraim, the youngest, and his left hand on Manasseh, the oldest.[1] Once again, Jacob/Israel is turning the tables on the tradition! What is it about him that makes him refuse to play by the rules? When Joseph tries to correct his father's error, Jacob/Israel tells him that he knows what he is doing: the younger will be greater than

---

[1] See "A Blessing Wrought in Deception (Gen 27.1-10; 28.2-4)."

Israel Blesses the Sons of Joseph (Gen 48.15-16, 20)

the older. Maybe we are to understand from this that God's blessing do not always come the way we might think, or want, or to whom we might prefer.

Meaning

Jesus, many centuries later, tells a story of a man with two sons, the younger of which demands his inheritance early. He runs off and spends it all on wild living, while the older one stays at home, being responsible, and waiting for his time. When the younger son, destitute and shamed, returns home, the father welcomes him with a lavish feast. The older one is bothered by this celebration, and asks his father why he has done such a thing. He, the eldest, has done everything he should and has not received a banquet. The father is compassionate but points out that the eldest has always had everything from the father. The younger one, however, was lost and has now returned, repentant.[2] It may sometimes bother us how God does things, but He cares about everyone, and He has a plan. Perhaps a more positive way to think about it is this: God is always capable of surprising us. Be careful what you pray for!

In most modern cultures, we use Wills and Trusts to pass along inheritance rather than near-death blessings. Yet the structure of this blessing can be a model for our blessings—maybe even on our own children or grandchildren.

---

[2] Luke 15.11–32.

The blessing begins with an extensive introduction describing God as the One who walked with Jacob/Israel's ancestors, the One who shepherded him all his life, and as the Angel who redeemed him from harm. This blessing begins by recalling all the good things God has done for the one praying.

Next, Jacob/Israel offers a blessing on the boys. He is passing on the same blessings that he received (in deceit) from his father Isaac, which were the same ones that Isaac received from his father, Abraham. "In them let my name be perpetuated, and the name of my ancestors Abraham and Isaac; and let them grow into a multitude on the earth."

Application

Since many of us offer petitions far more often than blessings, you might try choosing a day to *only* offer blessings. All the types of prayer are important, of course, and each adds richness and meaning to our prayer lives. Yet focusing on one type of prayer is a wonderful way to learn it well—especially the ones we tend to neglect. Review the other blessings in Genesis that we have studied so far in Genesis. Note the structure and the content, and put together your own model, or choose one to imitate during your "day of blessings." If you would like to stretch your "prayer muscles," ask someone to allow you to lay your hands on them as you pray a blessing on them.

Write in your journal about the experience of a day of blessings.

A Brief Prayer of Trust in God by Jacob (Gen 49.18)

"For your salvation I wait, Lord."

The final prayer in the book of Genesis is quite brief. Though we might think that the best prayers have some heft to them, there is no reason to believe that short prayers cannot be powerful as well. If prayer is about relationship, then the communication should be diverse: sometimes profound, sometimes simple; sometimes lengthy, sometimes short. I might pass my wife in the kitchen and say, "You look beautiful." I might have a moment between business meetings and say, "God, thank you for caring for me." When you have a little time between work tasks, family responsibilities, or any brief space of time, use the short prayers of the Bible as a model (we will see that there are many).

Background

In this prayer, Jacob/Israel says, "For your salvation I wait, Lord." Despite the brevity, it sums up much of the story and meaning of Genesis. The main characters in the book often demonstrate their lack of trust in God. Sometimes they acted out of fear and did not trust God to protect them (Abraham said, "she's my sister, not my wife" to protect himself). Sometimes they acted with selfishness (Isaac tricks his old father out of inheritance).[1] Sometimes, they are unwilling to wait for God's plan to unfold as He wills (Abraham having a child with Hagar),[2] and some even betrayed and imprisoned their own family members (Joseph's older brothers).[3] In other words, they are us. We lack faith and trust in God when things get tough; we try to make things happen on our own, and we betray and hurt others.

Meaning

Maybe, instead of "wait on the Lord," we prefer the saying, "God helps those who help themselves." That phrase does not appear in the Bible, yet that attitude is what gave Abram, Sarai, Hagar, and Ishmael so much heartache and suffering. The attitude of "waiting on the Lord" is an important one, and we will encounter it many times in our journey through the prayers of the Bible.

---

[1] See "A Blessing Wrought in Deception (Gen 27.7, 12–13, 27–29; 28.2–4)."
[2] See "Hagar's Lament and Petition (Gen 21.16)."
[3] See "Israel's Prayer for his Son's Success (Gen 43.14)."

A Brief Prayer of Trust in God by Jacob (Gen 49.18)

Through the long story of Jacob/Israel, we watch him grow in maturity and faith. From a young, selfish, conniving scoundrel to a strong, faithful patriarch, he learns to trust God completely. He knows Who controls the universe. He knows where his hope lies. What an excellent attitude to adopt: just rest and trust in the care of God! Jacob/Israel still had his weak moments, for sure, like all of us. But in this prayer, his character, faith, and maturity shine forth.

Jacob/Israel has learned that he must trust and wait, regardless of what his fears tell him. Salvation comes from God, and it comes when He decides. This can be difficult to accept, maybe more so in a world where so many things come fast: food, phone calls, text messages, news, cash, and so on. In general, we are not patient people, and it follows that we may not be good at waiting for God. Perhaps we are no worse than those of the ancient world: fifty times in scripture we are urged to do just that: "wait on the Lord."

Application

This is an easy prayer to incorporate into our daily lives. A prayer with an opening, a body, and a closing is useful, helpful, and proper. But a prayer does not have to have those elements or a lot of words. Look over the fourteen prayers we have examined in Genesis. Use what you have learned and write down two or three short prayers you could use in your own prayers. Try rewriting the prayers if they are too long; capture the purpose of the prayer in just one sentence. See if you can come up with one short prayer for each type of prayer in Genesis: a petition, a blessing, a vow, and an intercession. As an alternative, you might take this prayer of Jacob/Israel's and use it whenever you have a brief moment. Look it up in different Bible translations. Choose the one you like, or mix and match. Offer it as a prayer, to remind you to slow down and to wait for God's plan to unfold, rather than trying to force your own plan on Him.

Summary of the Prayers in Genesis

We have explored, studied, and prayed the prayers in Genesis. These prayers show a lot of variety: five blessings, five petitions, two intercessions, two vows, and one each of a thanksgiving, a lament, and a curse.

This variety is not in the *types* of prayers, it is among the people who offer them: men and women, old and young, noble and common, and even believers and nonbelievers. The form and structure of the prayers are also diverse. Some are short, others quite long; some are formal, whole others are quite informal; some are complex, some are simple. Even the circumstances of the prayers vary: birth, marriage, death, danger, suffering, celebration, and success. That is, the areas of life which touch us all in some way. What richness of prayer we find—and we have only studied the first book of the Bible!

Five of these prayers are blessings: prayers offered to God asking him to bless someone. The people who offer such prayers are Noah, a pagan priest, an Israelite slave, parents of a young girl, an old father who offers the blessing because he has been deceived, and an old patriarch. Who are these blessings bestowed upon? Four of the five are blessings upon children by parents. Noah, Isaac, and Jacob bless their sons before they die and Rebekah's parents bless her before she gets married. Maybe those of us who are parents should practice this more often and with more intention.

Five petitions match the five blessings. A slave asks God to lead him to the right wife for his master; wives pray for children; and a man on a journey, kicked out of his home, prays for safety and protection.

There are two intercessions: one is on behalf of an unbeliever that nothing bad will happen to him. The other is a prayer for children as they go off on a dangerous journey.

Vows are mentioned twice; both are by the same man. Once, when he is young and selfish, he makes a vow to God to worship him if God will take care of him. As an older man, he promises to that he will do whatever God requires of him.

There is only one thanksgiving in Genesis, though we will see many more of these in other books of the Bible. This one is offered by a servant who has succeeded in the task given to him by his master.

There is also one lament: a parent to cries out to God as she and her child are dying in the desert. Along with the blessings is one curse—also from a parent to a child who dishonored the parent.

If the first fourteen prayers of the Bible show a great richness in type, should that richness not also show in our own prayer lives?

Exodus

Introduction

Exodus means "going out," and this book describes how the people of Israel "went out" into the world to become a nation of their own. Four hundred years have passed since the events at the end of Genesis, and the descendants of Israel have gone from being guests to slave workers. This is the story of how they turned back to God, and how He delivered them and made them His people.

The prayers in Exodus do not show as much variety as the prayers in Genesis. It may be because the book revolves around one major event (the Exodus) and because most of them involve some issue of suffering or a response to it. Still, there are petitions, intercessions, praise prayers, and a blessing—some of the most common types in the Bible.

After the great variety of prayer in Genesis, Exodus allows us to learn more about prayer by concentrating on a few types. It also introduces us to the concept of how the different prayer types flow from and to one another.

The Israelites Cry Out for Help (Exod 2.23)

The Israelites groaned under their slavery, and cried out. Out of the slavery their cry for help rose up to God. God heard their groaning, and God remembered his covenant with Abraham, Isaac, and Jacob. God looked upon the Israelites, and God took notice of them.

Background

The first prayer in the book of Exodus is a brief mention, but it is filled with pathos. It is the story of a deep cry to God—a cry that does not come in the form of a structured petition or with traditional phrases and invocations. It is a cry that flows out of pain and suffering. It is the cry of a dying child in the night, the sobbing of a prisoner in a cell, the wail of a woman who has lost her husband. It is not the cry of one person; it is the cry of an entire people. Think of Jews in Nazi Germany, those remaining in a medieval town after the Black Plague, or the suffering families in Dufar of the early twenty-first century.

Though the Israelites began as guests of Pharaoh at the time of Joseph, four hundred years have passed, and their situation has changed. The Pharaohs of Egypt no longer "recognize" the Israelites as special people—they are just foreigners. (There is some historical evidence that the Pharaoh at the time of Joseph may have been from a group of non-Egyptians who had taken over Egypt. When the Egyptians reconquered the land, the Israelites, being foreigners, were treated as unwelcome aliens). These new Pharaohs engaged in massive building projects of temples, pyramids, statues, palaces, and even entire cities. It took a lot of money, and much of it, at first, came from taxing the citizens. When that was not enough, each citizen was required to work for the Pharaoh for one month a year in return for food and board. Finally, when more labor was needed, the Pharaohs enslaved vulnerable groups such as resident aliens. The Israelites were just such a group. They were conscripted as slaves to help build two massive storehouse cities: Pithom (modern Tell el-Rataba) and Rameses (modern Tell ed-Dab'a).

The suffering of slaves under the hot sun and the heavy labor led the foremen to go to the Egyptian overlords and ask for better conditions. The response was to make things even more difficult.

It had been centuries since the Israelites had leaders such as Jacob/Israel and Joseph. The opening chapters of Exodus show that the people may have forgotten their history with God and the practices of their ancestors. If we read through all of Genesis and into Exodus, we notice that it has been a long time since we have read much about God's care for his people. Maybe they did not know about the special relationship with God that their

The Israelites Cry Out for Help (Exod 2.23)

ancestors had. Maybe they knew nothing about those fourteen important prayers we examined in the last section.

They did know something about God, though, and they cry out to Him. They "groaned under their slavery" and cried in out in prayer. The word translated "groaned" is a word that can mean a "deep sigh," but it has other meanings, too. Here, it probably refers to the kind of groan a person might utter under physical distress. Imagine a team of cattle as they struggle and groan trying to pull a heavy cart up a mountain, or a horse that has been ridden too long and too hard. The Israelites are like cattle—mistreated, pushed beyond their limits with no one to stand up for them.

But God hears their cry. Even though there has been almost no mention of God's care to this point in the book of Exodus, the following verses show that God knows their situation (vv24-25). He "remembers" the covenant he made with Abraham, Isaac, and Jacob.

Meaning

Throughout these stories, the writers never mention the names of the Egyptian kings, just "Pharaoh" (the Egyptian word for a king-like leader). We can assume the writer(s) knew their names. *We* know the names, though not from the Bible, but from the Egyptians (who kept excellent records). The Pharaoh was either Thutmose III or Rameses II. Why do the writers not name them? They mention God, Abraham, Isaac, Jacob, and later, Moses and Aaron—but not a single name of any Pharaoh, magician, assistant, or priest.

In the world's eyes, a person has value if they have status, power, or money. In God's eyes, a person has value because God created that person. Unlike the book of Exodus, the beginning of the Gospel of Luke mentions several important Roman leaders: Herod, Augustus, and Quirinius, along with their status, roles, and accomplishments. These, according to the world, are the people who matter. Yet after Luke names those people and their positions, he turns to an entire story about "nobodies." An unimportant priest named Zechariah, a poor young Jewish teen with no status or power (Mary), and her soon-to-be-husband, Joseph. The rest of the story is about their children (John and Jesus) who will change the world forever and fulfill God's plans for salvation. What matters to the world is rarely the same as what is important to God. The writer of Exodus is doing the same as Luke in a different way: in God's world, it is not the political leaders of Egypt that matter, but those who follow Him and care for His people.

This brief but heartfelt petition of these Israelite slaves teaches us a something about our petitions. First, even though it may sometimes seem like God has forgotten us, He knows—even if you have forgotten Him. Second, it is not always necessary to pray with using specific structures or words. Even a genuine cry as a prayer is appropriate—perhaps most suitable in some situations. Finally, God keeps his promises. It appeared that, after four hundred years, He had forgotten about His people. He had not—his timetable is not our timetable. Though He did not stop the Israelites from becoming slaves, and even though they would wander the desert for forty years in the wilderness, they did eventually enter the Promised

The Israelites Cry Out for Help (Exod 2.23)

Land. They matured a lot along the way and learned a lot about themselves and God.

Application

When we are suffering in some way, perhaps crying out is the best prayer we can offer. Like a child crying to a parent, a puppy for its mother, or a lost soul for direction. Regardless of whether the reasons is loneliness, or the despair of life, or am unknown future, this Parent cares and listens. Trust that He will keep his promises, and "wait on the Lord."

If you are not currently suffering, you might think of a time when you were, or when someone else was, and a "crying out" was appropriate. What happened? Has God responded yet? Or was there more waiting to do?

Moses Offers a Prayer on Behalf of Pharaoh (Exod 8.8-9, 12)

Then Pharaoh called Moses and Aaron, and said, "Pray to the LORD to take away the frogs from me and my people, and I will let the people go to sacrifice to the LORD." Moses said to Pharaoh, "Kindly tell me when I am to pray for you and for your officials and for your people, that the frogs may be removed from you and your houses and be left only in the Nile."

Then Moses and Aaron went out from Pharaoh; and Moses cried out to the LORD concerning the frogs that he had brought upon Pharaoh.

Background

The second prayer in Exodus is the third intercession that appears the Bible. Moses offered this prayer on behalf of the Egyptian Pharaoh. It takes place after the second of the ten plagues brought on the Egyptians by God.

Moses, directed by God, goes before the Pharaoh to ask that the Israelites be allowed to go out into the desert to worship and sacrifice to their God. Before Moses appears before the Pharaoh, God tells him what will happen. The Pharaoh will refuse, which will allow God to reveal his power, both to the Israelites and to the Egyptians. God needs to re-introduce Himself to the Israelites, but He also wants the Egyptians to know that He is the one, true God (7:5). Despite the way this story ends for the Egyptians, God is not primarily concerned about punishment, but about giving people the opportunity to come to Him.

The events at the palace unfold just as God described. The Pharaoh refuses to let the Israelites go out into the desert to worship. Again directed by God, Moses and Aaron perform some miracles to show the power of their God. The Pharaoh is not impressed and directs his wizards perform similar, if less impressive, feats, to demonstrate the power of the Egyptian Gods. God then brings the first plague to the land, and the waters of Egypt becomes blood-red. Pharaoh's wizards perform a similar act, so the Pharaoh refuses to let the Israelites go.

Moses then repeats his demand. When Pharaoh refuses again, the second plague begins and frogs appear over the land. Though the wizards again perform a similar feat, the overwhelming inundation of the country by amphibians seems to weaken the Pharaoh's will. In the passage quoted above, he asks Moses to pray that the plague end. Moses asks whether he will allow Israelites to go worship. The Pharaoh tells him that they can go worship their God the following day. Moses agrees. He leaves the palace and "cried" out to the Lord about the frogs. The word translated as "cried" is the Hebrew word *yitzach*,

Moses Offers a Prayer on Behalf of Pharaoh (Exod 8.8-9, 12)

which means "to cry for help," "to cry out in need," or just "to cry out in prayer."

God answers immediately. The frogs die, and the people gathered them up and burn them. True to form, when everything is back to normal, the Pharaoh becomes stubborn and refuses to let the Israelites go—as he would do eight more times.

Meaning

We have encountered two other prayers of intercession in our journey through the Bible's prayers. The first was by Abraham. He prayed that nothing bad would happen to Abimelech after he took Sarah because he did not know she was Abraham's wife.[1] There are similarities between that prayer and this one. Both were offered for a nonbeliever; both were offered at the request of the nonbeliever; both were requests for relief from punishment by God. The second intercession in the Bible was the prayer offered by Jacob/Israel for his sons as they headed back to Egypt for food and to attempt to rescue their brother Simeon.[2] Though that prayer is not as similar as the first, there are connections with Egypt, an Egyptian leader, and the fear of suffering or even death.

What do we learn about intercessions from these prayers? First, we see that it is not uncommon for biblical

---

[1] See "Abraham Intercedes for Abimelech (Gen 20.7, 17)."
[2] See "Israel's Prayer for his Son's Success (Gen 43.14)."

characters to pray on behalf of an unbeliever who is suffering. We might think such a prayer would ask for the unbeliever to become a follower of God. Yet two of the three intercessions we have studied pray for God to relieve their suffering, even though they are not believers.

Second, this intercession indicates something mysterious about intercessory prayer. God already knew the Pharaoh would be stubborn—he told Moses so. We assume that God even knew that Pharaoh would go back on his promise once He relieved the land of the frogs. Yet God heeded the prayer for the Pharaoh anyway. Most of us would do no such thing: if we *knew* someone was going to back out on a promise once we gave in, we would probably not give in. In fact, we often refuse to give in to others if we only suspect they will go back on their word.

This is not how God operates. He is always about second chances—and third chances, and fourth chances, and so on. Of course, God has his limits (after the tenth time in this story, for instance). Unlike us, God generously offers chances for redemption, chances to do the right thing, and chances to turn ourselves around. God goes to ridiculous lengths for someone like the Pharaoh, long after a human would have given up.

The Pharaoh was never able to do the right thing. That doesn't mean that someone that we pray for might not turn around. Their response is not our concern—it is God's business and their business. Our obligation is to intercede for them—not only so they will come to follow God, but that their life will be free of suffering and deliverance from pain.

Moses Offers a Prayer on Behalf of Pharaoh (Exod 8.8-9, 12)

Application

Think of a few people that you know who are not believers. Maybe they are even hostile towards you or your faith. Choose one who has some difficulty or suffering. Pray for them—not only that they will "see the light," but that relief from suffering or difficulty will come. God cares about them, too. Who knows? Maybe through your prayer not only will they be healed, but that healing might lead them to God. Either way, it is our role to offer intercessory prayers for both believers and nonbelievers.

Moses Prays Again for the Pharaoh
(Exod 9.28-29, 33)

Pray to the LORD! Enough of God's thunder and hail! I will let you go; you need stay no longer." Moses said to him, "As soon as I have gone out of the city, I will stretch out my hands to the LORD; the thunder will cease, and there will be no more hail, so that you may know that the earth is the LORD'S.

So Moses left Pharaoh, went out of the city, and stretched out his hands to the LORD...

Background

Moses offers another intercession for the Pharaoh. This time, it is after the seventh plague, a powerful hailstorm. The previous intercession was offered, at the request of the Pharaoh, after the second plague of frogs. Since then, there have been gnats, flies, a deadly livestock pestilence, and painful boils on humans and animals. After the sixth, a subtle word change takes place in the story. Subtle, but powerful in meaning.

After each of the first five plagues, Pharaoh "hardened" or "strengthened" his heart (two different Hebrew words are used, though not all translations make that clear). It means that Pharaoh chose to be stubborn or was at the mercy of his pride.

Starting with the next plague, however, there is a shift in the subject of the verb. No longer does the text say that *Pharaoh* made his heart stubborn; rather, it is *God* making the Pharaoh's heart stubborn. Does this mean that God was *forcing* the Pharaoh go against Him so He can then punish him? That seems unfair, but remember, God gave the Pharaoh many chances (the original request and each time after the plagues). God even granted the prayer of Moses on the Pharaoh's behalf after the second plague. Still, the Pharaoh continues to insist on his own way. God is patient, generous, and forgiving—but there is a limit. God is not like a parent who lets their children do anything they want, nor a parent ready to criticize or punish at first instance. God offers opportunity after opportunity for us to do the right thing *on our own*. At some point, though, if we continue to insist on our own way, He will let us go—we do have free will. Sometimes, as in the case of the Pharaoh, He will even use our stubbornness for a larger purpose (which may work against us). Paul describes this idea in theological terms in Romans 1.20-27. Though people know God in many ways—through His Word, through prophets, through nature—if they continue in their stubbornness, ignoring Him and the created purpose of life, He will "give them over" to their sinful ways. A dire warning! This is not to say the person is lost forever. God

Moses Prays Again for the Pharaoh (Exod 9.28-29, 33)

would *still* welcome them back with open arms if they repented. Paul engages in long argument through the next seven chapters of Romans showing that *all of us* are in need of redemption and unable to obtain it on our own. He writes "thanks be to God" because Jesus has opened the way for redemption, no matter how stubborn in sin we were (Rom 7.25-8.39).

Meaning

It may disturb us that God would turn our stubbornness against us and use it for His purposes. But it is our choice. After all, we can choose to be part of His "team" or the opposing "team." Like the Pharaoh, if we continue to insist on our own way and selfish purposes, without a care to God or others, we run that risk.

Even here we see that there is still hope for the stubborn. Despite God's use of the Pharaoh's stubbornness against him, Moses prayed for the Pharaoh *again*. Moreover, God answers the prayer. God is still giving the Pharaoh a chance to change his ways. This is not only a sign of God's unquenchable willingness to offer second chances but it also of the efficacy of intercessory prayer—no matter how stubborn and hopeless someone might be. There are no "lost causes" for God.

After the prayer, the Pharaoh repents. He tells Moses, "I have sinned" (9.27). At first, Moses does not believe him, despite his seeming sincerity. He probably was sincere—a man who lived in the moment, felt responsible for the terrible things that happened, but later allowed pride take over. Do we not do the same? We forget how bad we felt after the suffering is over and the pain has receded into the past. How many vows have we made and not kept?

In the previous prayer, we focused on the importance of praying for others, no matter who they are, believer or nonbeliever. This prayer emphasizes that same point, but it also encourages us to look at our *own* needs for intercession. Maybe others are praying for us and we, like the Pharaoh, are being stubborn. Maybe we think we are right; maybe we are afraid to admit we are wrong; maybe we are protecting our egos.

Application

It is helpful for us to spend some time realizing that there are probably other people interceding for us. We can pray that our stubbornness does not get in the way of those intercessory prayers being answered.

Can you think of someone who might be interceding for you? Do you have a stubbornness that might keep those prayers from succeeding? This can be difficult. It is not easy to question our beliefs or approaches to life. But we can always pray for humility, and pray that God will break down our obstinacy when necessary.

Moses Offers a Third Prayer for the Pharaoh
(Exod 10.17-18)

"...Do forgive my sin just this once, and pray to the LORD your God that at the least he remove this deadly thing from me." So he went out from Pharaoh and prayed to the LORD.

Background

After the plague of a hailstorm pounds Egypt with a vengeance, the familiar pattern of discourse between Moses and the Pharaoh repeats. Now (as noted in the last chapter), it is *God* who is causing the Pharaoh to be stubborn. God gave him five chances to do the right thing; Pharaoh refused each time. After that, God used the Pharaoh's stubbornness against him to show God's mighty power over creation. It may seem that God had "given up" on Pharaoh, but He has not. He grants Moses' prayers for the Pharaoh twice during the next five plagues.

This prayer comes after the ninth plague: locusts. These terrible pests strip the land of all vegetation.

The Pharaoh's advisors tell him to let these Israelites go before they destroy Egypt. But his stubbornness gets the best of him yet again, and he refuses. The plague comes, and the locusts eat everything left after the destruction wrought by the hail.

Again, the Pharaoh is repentant. "I have sinned," he says once more. He asks for forgiveness and for Moses to pray for him again. Once more, God hears the prayer and the locusts go away. Yet, as we have come to expect, God makes the Pharaoh stubborn once more. It will be the last time.

Meaning

As noted in the previous chapter, it seems unfair of God to *make* the Pharaoh stubborn even after he admits that he has sinned. God forces the king of Egypt to resist Him so that God can then punish him. Yet once the Pharaoh relents (after the tenth plague) and agrees to let the Israelites go, God brings an *eleventh* plague upon Egypt— the most horrific of all. Egypt could recover from the other plagues, but this one involved the death of every firstborn human and animal. Doesn't this seem vengeful? God has won, after all. Why kill children?

There may not be satisfying answer to this question for us, but there is a reason for it. God is demonstrating his sovereignty. The lesson is that continued stubbornness against him can lead to disastrous results. He is the Creator and Sustainer of *everything*, he is in charge of everything; therefore he can do anything he wants. We might cry, "unfair!" but that would be like telling an artist that he cannot scrub out a section of his painting and

Moses Offers a Third Prayer for the Pharaoh (Exod 10.17-18)

redo it, or telling an author she cannot delete a paragraph. We might think the artist was wrong, and we might criticize, but we should be able to admit that it is the artist's work to do with as the artist pleases. Job affirmed this about God when he says, "The Lord gives and the Lord takes away, blessed be the name of the Lord" (Job 1.21). It is what Malachi meant when he writes that the Lord loved Jacob (Israel), but he hated Esau (the Edomites) in 1.2-3. It is what Paul meant when he quotes that passage in Romans 9.13.

Prayer is not about getting God to do what we want. He is not a divine Santa Claus. Nor he is a distant Zeus who sits on high and hurls lightning bolts. He is unique in his person and dealings with us.

Think about some of the best parents you know. They have certain characteristics in common: they love their children and show it; they have the children's best interests in mind; they have clear guidelines for acceptable and unacceptable behavior; they practice consistent consequences for violating those guidelines; they are always willing to forgive and forget once the children confess and repent. They are parents that always offer second chances, and never connect the punishment of a child with the value of a child. They are good parents because they are mimicking God in many ways, who is the model of the perfect parent.

God *wanted* the Pharaoh to relent. He *wanted* the Pharaoh to have a relationship with Him. Even when the Pharaoh continued to reject God and continued hurt God's children, God continued to give him a chance to change. But the Pharaoh is not God's only child. When it came time to choose between the well-being of the Israelites over the Pharaoh, God acted with decisiveness and justice. Though it may seem unfair for God to force the Pharaoh to be stubborn, two things may help us understand. First, we do not see the whole picture as God does; we have no overarching view of history and the universe. So we need to trust that He knows what He is doing. Second, the problem did not begin with God—the problem is those who continually refuse Him and hurt others in spite of His mercy.

When we offer intercessions for others, we should remember those characteristics. God desires all people to be in a relationship with Him. He is the ultimate Creator and can do whatever he wants—but he offers us the opportunity to be a part of it all. This powerful, sovereign, terrifying God, says to us, "come and be with me…tell me what you think…be a part of my Plan." When we offer prayers for others, this is what we do—we become part of God's plans. Scripture indicates that it is possible for us to influence God (see Genesis 18, for instance). Maybe, because God knows everything and we don't, He will not take our advice. Sometimes He will do as we ask. But the great gift is that we are allowed to be part of it.

At the time of Paul of Tarsus, the Emperors of Rome had a circle of friends and family that he consulted for advice while he ruled the Empire. They were not officials, but they were the closest people to him. They were called the "Friends of Caesar." Believers are part of the "Friends of God" when we intercede for others—we are giving Him our input.

Moses Offers a Third Prayer for the Pharaoh (Exod 10.17-18)

Application

This image is helpful as we work to enrich our prayer lives. When you offer intercessions, imagine yourself going up to God's palace. When the guards challenge you, you say "I am a Friend of God." The guards bow, lower their weapons and allow you to pass. Enter the hall and sit before God on his throne, and tell Him what you think about these others on whose behalf you pray.

A Prayer-Hymn of Praise (Exod 15.1-18)

"I will sing to the LORD, for he has triumphed gloriously;
 horse and rider he has thrown into the sea.
  The LORD is my strength and my might,
   and he has become my salvation;
  this is my God, and I will praise him,
   my father's God, and I will exalt him.
  The LORD is a warrior;
   the LORD is his name.

"Pharaoh's chariots and his army he cast into the sea;
 his picked officers were sunk in the Red Sea.
  The floods covered them;
   they went down into the depths like a stone.
  Your right hand, O LORD, glorious in power—
your right hand, O LORD, shattered the
  enemy.
  In the greatness of your majesty you overthrew

> *your adversaries;*
> *you sent out your fury, it consumed them like stubble.*
> *At the blast of your nostrils the waters piled up,*
> *the floods stood up in a heap;*
> *the deeps congealed in the heart of the sea.*
> *The enemy said, 'I will pursue, I will overtake,*
> *I will divide the spoil, my desire shall have its*
> *fill of them.*
> *I will draw my sword, my hand shall destroy them.'*
> *You blew with your wind, the sea covered them;*
> *they sank like lead in the mighty waters.*
>
> *"Who is like you, O LORD, among the gods?*
> *Who is like you, majestic in holiness,*
> *awesome in splendor, doing wonders?*
> *You stretched out your right hand,*
> *the earth swallowed them.*
>
> *"In your steadfast love you led the people whom you redeemed;*
> *you guided them by your strength to your holy abode.*
> *The peoples heard, they trembled;*
> *pangs seized the inhabitants of Philistia.*
> *Then the chiefs of Edom were dismayed;*

A Prayer-Hymn of Praise (Exod 15.1-18)

> *trembling seized the leaders of Moab;*
> *all the inhabitants of Canaan melted away.*
> *Terror and dread fell upon them;*
> *by the might of your arm, they became still as a stone*
> *until your people, O LORD, passed by,*
> *until the people whom you acquired passed by.*
> *You brought them in and planted them on the mountain of your own possession,*
> *the place, O LORD, that you made your abode,*
> *the sanctuary, O LORD, that your hands have established.*
> *The LORD will reign forever and ever."*

In this book, I have drawn a distinction between prayers of praise and prayers of thanksgiving, though they are similar. It might even be difficult to tell them apart at times because some prayers contain both. As described in the Introduction, we offer prayers of thanksgiving as a prayer that *thanks* God for some act or acts. Just you might thank someone for answering a request, or helping you, or giving you a gift, so we are grateful to God for things he does.

A prayer of praise, on the other hand, praises God for who He is. Its focus is on God's character. We praise Him for His power, for his magnificent acts of creation, for His past acts of salvation, or for being the kind of God who forgives. We might say to a friend, "you are really good at listening," or to a parent, "I love the way you take care of me," or to a co-worker, "you have wonderful speaking skills." Just as we might offer a word of praise to someone as a general comment on their person or character, we do the same to God.

You can see why categorizing these prayers might be difficult: how is praising God for creation different from thanking him for it? How is thanking him for past acts of salvation different from thanking him for them? The difference is in the focus (and perhaps timeframe). I offer a prayer of thanksgiving because he saved *me*; I would offer praise to him because *He* is the kind of God who saves people. Subtle, perhaps, but the distinction can help us think through what we are praying and give us more richness and clarity in our prayers.

Background

This prayer (which is in the form of a hymn) is a prayer of praise, but it does contain a few lines that are thanking God for deliverance from the Egyptians. Most of it, though, praises God because he is the God who can and does deliver. The focus is on what God does, not what happened to the Israelites.

The context is that the Israelites have been delivered from their Egyptian slavery. After all the suffering, the plagues, the frustrating back-and-forth with the Pharaoh, they are free. In the well-known story, God parts the Red Sea, allowing the Israelites to pass through in safety. As their enemies close in behind them, God closes the Sea, destroying or stopping the Egyptian troops and saving the Israelites.

When the Israelites reach the opposite shore, having seen the extraordinary power of God over creation and

A Prayer-Hymn of Praise (Exod 15.1-18)

Egypt, Moses and the Israelites offer a prayer about God's power, rather than a "thank you."

Meaning

Of course, a praise includes the implication of a thanksgiving. Consider this: someone opens a door for you, and you say, "Thank you." At work, someone presents you with a lovely gift, and you say, "Thank you." Later that day, your car breaks down, and someone stops along the road and gives your battery a charge, and you say, "Thank you." "Thank you" is an appropriate response to those particular acts of kindness.

Now imagine this scene: you are dying in a hospital and need a kidney transplant. A volunteer offers to donate one of her kidneys. The doctors determine she is a match, and they perform the surgery with success. The fear of death turns into the joy of life. After the surgery, would you turn to the donor and say, "thank you," as if they had given you a place in line or changed a tire for you? Most of us would feel the need to do more, even if it was just, "You are so selfless!" or "You are a lifesaver!" In such situations, our focus turns from the act itself to person who did it. Instead of "thank you for *giving* me this *gift*," or "thank you for helping me *fix my tire*," we are saying "*you* are such a generous person," or "*your actions* are above and beyond what most would do." Praise is offered when someone has gone far beyond a gift or a helping hand to the point where the focus should be on them, not just the act they performed. We turn our attention from what we have received or what the other person has given to the quality of the one who sacrificed.

This is what prayers of praise do. They *celebrate* the giver. They move beyond gratitude to *praise*. It helps us draw a distinction between a nice gesture and a life-changing action. If we think about the giver for a moment, we can understand how appropriate that is. When someone opens a door for you, gives you a place in line, or even buys you a gift, they have done something kind, but they have not sacrificed much. It may or may not say anything about their character. But someone who *sacrifices* for you demonstrates the quality of their person.

This is why the Israelites respond with this beautiful hymn of praise to God. Note the focus on the character and actions of God. *He* has triumphed, *He* is strength and might and salvation; *He* is a warrior. The hymn recounts what God did to free the Israelites, and little about the Israelites themselves. "No one is like you!" they sing.

Application

Here is another way we can enrich our prayers. For one day, try praying only prayers of praise. It is easy to stray into thanksgiving, and, of course, there is nothing wrong with that. But it is a good discipline, at times, to practice *only* praise, because it helps us in two ways. First, it moves the focus from ourselves and onto God. Second, it helps us to appreciate anew the incredible God that we worship for more than just what he has done for us.

Miriam and the Women Praise God
(Exod 15.21)

Sing to the LORD, for he has triumphed gloriously;
horse and rider he has thrown into the sea.

The followers of God have been putting their prayers to music since the beginning. The book of Psalms is a collection of hymns that were sung by the Israelites and Jews at worship (unfortunately, only the lyrics have survived).[1] Here are a few other examples from Scripture:

- Deborah and Barak sang a prayer together of thanks and praise to God after victory in battle (Judges 5)
- Jesus and his disciples sing the standards hymns that we sing after Passover (Mt 26.30; Mk 14.26)

---

[1] Some of the musical directions are found in the beginning of some Psalms. For example: instruments to use (Ps 5); the tune to use (Ps 8); a time to pause (Ps 52.5).

- James tells believers they are to sing prayers of praise (James 5.13)
- Revelation depicts people singing praises to God (Rev 4.8, 5.9, 14.3, 15.3).

Singing our prayers, in addition to speaking them and writing them, adds richness to the practice of prayer.

Background

The context of the present passage is Israel's deliverance through the Reed Sea (the "Red Sea"). It comes after the prayer in Exodus 15.1–18, and the reason for this prayer is the same as that one. After the long controversy with the Pharaoh about the Israelites slaves and the demonstration of God's power, the Israelites finally left Egypt. They march to the Reed Sea with a plan to continue east. But the Pharaoh changed his mind (again!) and chased after the Israelites with his army. The Israelites complain to Moses, and God opens the waters for them to pass through, destroying the following army in the muck and mire. On the other side, the Israelites erupt in a prayer of praise for God—not so much because he saved them (though that is part of it)—but because they are in awe of his power over creation. The previous prayer of praise is sung by "Moses and the Israelites" (Exodus 15.1). The Hebrew words might mean that all the Israelites sang together, or it could mean that it was just the men singing. When that hymn of praise ends, Miriam (the sister of Moses), takes a tambourine in her hand and leads the women of Israel in dancing and singing a hymn. We are only given a brief bit of the lyrics:

Miriam and the Women Praise God (Exod 15.21)

"Sing to the LORD, for he has triumphed gloriously; horse and rider he has thrown into the sea." Miriam was a religious leader of Israel along with her brother. In this passage, she is called a "prophetess" and leads the women in worship (see also Exodus 2.1–10 and Mic 6.4). With such a role in the community, it is natural for her to take part in leading the celebration. This entire scene sounds like a scene from our modern genre of a musical drama—after a significant event, the people break out in song! Moses and the men arise and sing their song of praise as a prayer to God, then they sit down, and the women rise to sing their version of the prayer.

Meaning

The two prayers of praise are a creative, heartfelt, and joyful responses to God's power over creation and what He did for the Israelites. Why sing them? Because sometimes spoken words alone are not enough. Most of us have experienced the power of music to express deep-felt emotions—more so than only spoken words. Many people have a song that they associate with important events in life (whether happy or melancholy). Decades later, those songs can bring tears to our eyes or a smile to our face. Music exists because God built it into creation and gave humans the ability to create it. In such acts of composing, playing, or singing music, we are mimicking the creative acts of God. He is the Master Composer and Performer. He has given us the ability to do the same under his power and direction. So it is only natural that music would be another way that we can enrich our prayers.

The next time you sing a hymn during worship, listen carefully to the lyrics. Most likely, you will find it is a prayer. Sing it like a prayer. During the week, at a time when you would pray, try singing a hymn or a Christian song in place of the spoken prayer. Keep that in mind as you listen and/or sing along: you are praying.

Application

You can use this idea of a prayer-hymn in a few different ways. If you are musical, you might write your own prayer-hymn. You could use some of the words from a Psalm for the lyrics (as has often been done throughout the centuries). If you like writing poetry or lyrics, try your hand at writing the words to a prayer-hymn. Imagine the Israelites at the Temple singing them, or later, singing them in synagogues, or the early Christians singing them in their home meetings.

During your devotional times this week, use one of these ideas for your prayers. Try singing all your prayers on one day: use hymns that fit your circumstance. Make up a melody or use an existing one for your prayers. Singing our prayers is another wonderful way to enrich our prayers because music speaks to us in a different way than spoken and written words. Singing our prayers is a way we can join with God in the creative activity which is a part of Him.

Jethro Blesses the Lord
(Exod 18.10)

"Blessed be the LORD, who has delivered you from the Egyptians and from Pharaoh."

Background

This passage contains a brief mention of a prayer of praise. You might read it and not even think of it as a prayer. It does not begin "Dear God." It does not have any formal prayer structure. It does not ask for anything. It contains no titles for God. It does not close with "amen." It is one sentence containing two phrases: "Blessed be the LORD, who has delivered you from the Egyptians and Pharaoh."

Yet it is no less a prayer than those which show more complexity or poetry. It is directed at God, it asks him to be "blessed," and it tells why God should be blessed. We might call this a "declaratory" prayer, or an "exclamatory" prayer. The word used here is translated as "blessed," but it does not have the same sense as when someone asks God to bless someone else. Otherwise, we would be asking God to bless Himself. Instead, the word here means "praise be to" or "may all people bless" God.

Meaning

Many prayers in the Bible use this word: it appears over four hundred times in the Old Testament alone. You might have heard this concept employed in modern ways. The most common is a response to a sneeze: "bless you!"[1] Perhaps you have heard it in the southern American phrase which usually denotes sympathy, "bless your heart!" But in ancient Hebrew, many nouns and verbs derive from the root of the word "blessing" (*brk*): words for praising or kneeling and praying. In the Bible, it is a word having to do with relationship between people or between people and God. The use of *brk* implies a favorable relationship, and is used to thank or praise someone for a material benefit or power that has been bestowed.

Often, a particular form of the verb is used when addressing God. What usually distinguishes it is that it implies a robust and meaningful relationship between the speaker and God. In other words, it is not just praising God for who He is (like most prayers of praise), it also acknowledges the goodwill that exists between God and the one praying. "I praise God for his mighty power, and we are traveling together in life: He loves me and helps me, and I love Him and offer Him my loyalty and service." It is praise, but it is an intimate praise. Imagine

---

[1] No one knows the origin of this practice, though there are plenty of theories related to the Black Plague; the mistaken idea that one's heart stops beating when sneezing; that your soul can be expelled when you sneeze; or that your body is trying to expel an evil spirit.

Jethro Blesses the Lord (Exod 18.10)

you are watching the news one night, and you hear a story in which a man gave a large sum of money to help a family who lost everything in a fire. You might exclaim, "what a generous, kind man!" That is praise, but it is formal and distant. Now, suppose you are part of the family who lost everything in that fire. When you say, "what a generous, kind man," it has a different meaning because of the relationship. Blessing God is praise with an emphasis on the relationship: it is less formal and more intimate. Both types of praise are appropriate for different times and circumstances.

In this passage, the father-in-law of Moses comes to meet him after the Israelites have been delivered from Egyptian slavery. This man is a bit of a biblical enigma. Here, his name is "Jethro," but in other places he is called "Reuel" (Exod 2.18; Num 10.29), and he may be the "Hobab" mentioned in Judges 4.11 (or "Hobab" might be Jethro's son). Not only was he Moses' father-in-law through his marriage to Zipporah, but he was also a priest of Midian. Was he a priest of Yahweh or a pagan god or goddess? It would seem strange if he were a priest of God since we learn in Exodus 6.3 that the Israelites had forgotten about God until Moses encountered Him as a burning bush. But why would a pagan priest be praising God? It is true that a pagan could believe in many gods and goddesses, and could choose to add God to the pantheon. What might be going on here?

Here's a good rule: if you read a passage and do not understand it, read everything before it and after it. The context will often provide a better understanding. Here, before Jethro offers this prayer, Moses tells him how God delivered the Israelites from slavery in Egypt. We can imagine him telling the whole story: the terrible suffering under their Egyptian masters, the audiences before the Pharaoh, the plagues, the Pharaoh's magicians, and finally the grand manner of their deliverance. When Moses finishes, Jethro rejoices "for all the good the Lord had done to Israel." Then, he pronounces the blessing-prayer above. As we noted above, blessings upon God involve some aspect of relationship. If Jethro was a pagan priest, would it be unlikely for him to use that term relationship-oriented prayer?

Perhaps that is the point of this prayer. Maybe, before Jethro hears the story, he believed in God as one among many, but not knowing about his real power and sovereignty. After his son-in-law tells him everything that happened, he understands that God is the One God. He is no distant deity nor shadowy spirit. He is a God who cares, who follows, who protects, and who delivers. Jethro becomes a true believer, and a blessing-prayer is now appropriate. He is a God who cares intimately about his people. Jethro's words after the prayer support this interpretation: "*Now I know* that the LORD is greater than all gods, because he delivered the people from the Egyptians."

Application

Prayer-blessings that have God as the subject are another type of prayer we can add to our growing list. This week, rather than offering standard prayers of praise or thanksgiving, offer some prayer-blessings. You might use Jethro's prayer as a model: begin with "blessed be the Lord" and then add your personal reason for why you are

Jethro Blesses the Lord (Exod 18.10)

offering the blessing. "Blessed be the Lord, who delivered me from a serious illness." As you pray in this way, remember that this type of prayer implies the close relationship you have with God, and the deep care he has for you. Keeping this in mind might lead you to use different words and terminology than the more formal prayers of praise.

Summary of the Prayers in Exodus

The book of Exodus does not have the same variety of prayers as Genesis. There is one petition, three intercessions, two prayers of praise, and a blessing. There is a reason for this: the book of Exodus revolves around a single major event which came to define the Israelites and still defines Jewish people today: the Exodus and the Passover. It also defines Christians: the Last Supper (The Lord's Supper, the Eucharist, Communion) was a Passover meal.

In many ways, Exodus is the other side of prayer from Genesis. Genesis depicts great number people in different situations and times. The prayers, therefore, are diverse in their type, in those who offer them, and in the circumstances. Genesis portrays prayer as used in many different areas of life. We see the richness of prayer in the stories of Genesis.

By contrast, Exodus focuses almost exclusively on Moses and the people he leads. It is focused on the Exodus itself, the events that led up to it, and some of the later events. The prayers are less diverse, and the underlying situation is almost the same in every prayer. It is prayer in a time of suffering, crisis, and deliverance.

The prayers in Exodus mirror the story itself. The first prayer is a petition: the Israelites cry out under the harsh yoke of Egyptian slavery. God hears them, and he gives them a leader in Moses and a way of deliverance. The next three prayers come during the plagues: all are intercessions for the Pharaoh, that God will forgive him and take away the plagues. Later, God brings the Israelites out of Egypt in a miraculous manner. On the far side of the Reed Sea, they offer praise-hymns to God: one for the men led by Moses, and one for the women, led by Miriam. The flow of these prayers matches a pattern we will see throughout many books of the Old Testament: prayers of petition and intercession lead to prayers of praise. We cry out, God acts, and we praise and thank him in return. This ebb and flow, the interrelated nature of prayer types, is an important part of the practice of prayer.[1]

---

[1] See the discussion of this idea in the Introduction.

Leviticus

Leviticus

Introduction

The book of Leviticus is a book of laws, not unlike books of laws which every country has written down somewhere. In most western countries (and many others), there are volumes (and online resources) that list criminal, civil, and governmental agency laws and regulations. There are also codebooks of "procedures" about how things are to be done in addition to the regular "substantive" laws). For instance, for a citizen to be arrested for robbing a bank (a crime under substantive law), the government officers and police must follow certain written rules, such as reading the arrestee his or her rights, filling out the proper paperwork, advising the right to an attorney (procedural law). If an employee wants to sue his employer for discrimination (substantive law), there are certain procedures that must be followed within a specific period of time, all described in the law (procedural law).

The book of Leviticus consists of a lot of procedural law—*how* the priests are to be chosen and initiated, *how* they priests are to carry out their jobs, how sacrifices are to be offered, and *for what things* they can be offered.

We might be surprised, therefore, to find out there is only one prayer in the book of Leviticus—and the words of the prayer are not even included, just a mention that a blessing was offered for all the people. But if we understand that most of this book is about procedure, we will realize that prayer is not procedural, it is substantive. More important, it is a spiritual practice which was part of Israelite life—it was not something new that God needed to lay down laws about. Prayer is about relationship, and does not require formality and a legal basis as did other acts (though it can have those, too).

You are not alone if you shy away from the book of Leviticus. It is no cause for shame because its genre makes for difficult reading. It lacks the drama of the stories in Genesis, the beautiful poetry of the Psalms, or the relevance of Paul's letters. Leviticus is mostly a set of instructions. Few people check out the Code of Civil Procedure from their local library for reading or study. Even attorneys do not read code books from front to back; they use them as a reference. To treat Leviticus as if it is a narrative to be read through from start to finish is to set yourself up for frustration. I have known many who vow to "read through the whole Bible from beginning to end" and do quite well until they arrive at Leviticus, where they get bogged down and give up.

Yet a Christian should read Leviticus at least once. The concepts of "sacrifice," "atonement," and the rituals found in Leviticus are crucial to a full understanding of the sacrifice of Jesus. Without that background, our understanding of the cross of Christ could be quite shallow. It would lack the historical and cultural depth that it would have had to Jews living at the time of Jesus.

I suggest you read Leviticus in sections, just as you would a reference book with which you wish to become familiar. The book is not in chronological order. The first seven chapters list and describe the five types of sacrifices, along with some instructions for the priests. Chapters 8–10 are about the institution of the priesthood, the ordination of the priests, and then closes with a short story that serves as a warning to the priests. The next seven chapters list issues of "cleanness" and "uncleanness"—the things that distinguish the Israelites as God's people from other people. Chapter 18–27 stress the need for dividing life into "holy spaces" in physical space as well as in time. Since the book is not in chronological order, there is no need to read it from front to back. It might be best to read the second part first (8-10) to learn about the purpose and roles of the priests. Then read about how God wished the Israelites to be set apart from other nations in their social, economic, and religious practices (18-27). You might then turn to the related issues of cleanness and uncleanness (11-17), and finish with the specific instructions on sacrifice (1-7). It is best to read each section in one sitting, so you don't miss the general structure and meaning and get lost in the details by reading it bits at a time. Reading it out loud can help your understanding as well (though you might get some strange looks from other people).

Aaron Blesses the People (Lev 9.22)

Aaron lifted his hands toward the people and blessed them...

Background

Leviticus contains instructions about the physical practices of community life, priesthood and sacrifices—not doctrines or spiritual practices. Though prayer was part of all sacrifices and many other areas of life, we learn about those when we read of the Israelites and priest doing these things, not in the instructions about them.

The lone prayer is found in a section that contains a narrative (chapters 8–10). The first part of this passage describes the ordination of Aaron and his sons as priests and the dedication of the Tabernacle and its altar. The second section describes the celebration on the eighth day: this is the story of the first time these practices were performed. First, the Tabernacle was cleansed with an offering. Then, the first sacrifice is offered as the beginning of the sacrificial tradition. Finally, the people shared a "sacred meal" in the presence of God. The prayer appears in the second section after Aaron has offered a sacrifice for himself and a second sacrifice for all the people. The story describes in detail how Aaron performed each part of the selection with care: slaughter, sacrifice, and the "cleaning up" activities—all stressing the importance of doing everything exactly as God commanded. After Aaron offers the sacrifice for the people, he lifts part of the sacrifice above his head and, holding it out to the people, he pronounces a blessing upon them. Fire comes from the altar and consumes the sacrifice, and the people fall to their knees and worship God.

Meaning

What can we learn about prayer from this passage? There are a few issues connected to the prayer-blessing: the importance of sacrifice, of doing things as God commands, and the importance of the people to God. Perhaps most important is never to take prayer lightly. In this story, prayer is connected to the most powerful acts of God as they relate to humans: forgiveness, atonement, blessing, and praise. Prayer is not just talking to yourself or talking out loud; it is not just meditation; it is not just a religious act. It is taking part in the very spirit of God. When you pray, especially when you offer a blessing on others, you are speaking *for* God! You stand as God's representative and bless what He blesses. You are His ambassador with your words. That is a task that should never be taken without serious thought.

Aaron Blesses the People (Lev 9.22)

Application

This week, as you pray, find a way to remind yourself of this powerful act you do. No matter how mundane and straightforward your prayer might seem, you are partaking in a way no less than Aaron himself. You speak with God Almighty and for God Almighty. You can even pray that you will remember that aspect of prayer—ask God to help you remember it—and thank him for allowing you to be His spokesperson.

Summary of the Prayer in Leviticus

The single prayer found in Leviticus comes in the midst of the story about the initiation of the system of priesthood and sacrifices. After Aaron prepares the first sacrifices, one for the priests and one for all the people, he pronounces a blessing upon the people. This act ties prayer his people: sacrifice, atonement, forgiveness, and reconciliation. The story reminds us that, although prayer can be spontaneous and informal, it is a great gift given to us by God. In the case of prayer-blessings, as in this passage, it makes us into ambassadors of God who speak for Him.

Numbers

Introduction

The book of Numbers contains prayers found within narrative sections, but it also contains a whole chapter of rules about a certain type of prayer. There are two intercessions, one blessing, a two-part petition, and a whole section of guidelines about offering prayer-vows.

The two blessings are part of the story of Israel wandering the desert and learning how to become the people of God. The first is the famous blessing of Numbers 6.24–26, which is often used as a benediction—a blessing on a congregation either at the beginning or end of a worship service. The second (the Prayer of the Ark) is a set of two petitionary prayers offered before and after a battle. Both of these prayers are excellent models of prayers to use at the beginnings and endings of events or times in our own lives.

There are two intercessions, both offered by Moses on behalf of the people who are suffering and complaining. These prayers show us some things about complaining and different ways God teaches us through prayer. Finally, there is a set of instructions about prayer-vows. This last section is difficult to understand and apply because it is rooted in ancient understandings of society, culture, and gender roles. Yet we can glean some important principles about how to offer prayer-vows.

The Lord Bless You and Keep You
(Num 6.24-26)

The LORD bless you and keep you;

*the LORD make his face to shine upon you,
and be gracious to you;*

*the LORD lift up his countenance upon you,
and give you peace.*

Background

This prayer is a blessing (sometimes called a "benediction" from a Latin word meaning "to speak well"). The one who speaks this prayer asks God to protect, favor, and grant peace to the person or persons who receive it.

It is first uttered during the Israelite's preparations for their march through the wilderness. The context, before and after the prayer, is of a unique nature for the Israelites. Much like the laws and the prayer in Leviticus, it is stressed that the Israelites belong to God; since He is holy, they must also be holy. In their daily lives they are to act, think, and speak with that in mind. This includes performing certain rituals to remind themselves of who they belong to, and to avoid things that defile the relationship with God. To be holy means to be "set apart." It is important to note that they are not "set apart, pure, and holy" because they keep the rules. Rather, they keep the rules because God has pronounced them "set apart, pure, and holy." In other words, God did not say "do these things and you will be holy," but "I have pronounced you holy—now go live like it." This is clear in the words that immediately follow the prayer: "they shall put my name on the Israelites, and I will bless them."

Meaning

This is a powerful and formal prayer, stating that God has adopted the Israelites as his people and that He will protect them, bless them, and give them peace. Moreover, God tells Moses that when the priests use this formula to bless the people, God will bless the people. (Again we see the concept of people being able to speak for God, like an ambassador.)

The triple use of the "personal" name of God in this prayer ("the LORD") also emphasizes its importance and its intimate nature. Those who can use this name are those who have the Name of God upon them. As we noted in the first prayer in Genesis,[1] the Hebrew word is YHWH, also know as the Tetragrammaton (the Four Letters). It is most likely a form of the Hebrew verb "to

---

[1] See "The Personal Name of God (Gen. 4.26)."

The Lord Bless You and Keep You (Num 6.24-26)

be"; many translations have "I Am" in its place. The word is not a general word *el* or *elohim* ("God"), nor is it a title like *el shaddai* ("God Almighty,") nor is it an address of respect like *adonai* ("Lord"). It is the "personal" name of God. In fact, as we noted in the first chapter, the name became so sacred to the Jews that, over time, that they refused to pronounce it out loud. For them, to speak it out loud was to desecrate it, to speak of God in the third person as if He were not present. It was not any name, a general name—it was the Name of God. Over those centuries, the vowels were forgotten, and we are left today with only the consonants "YHWH."

Furthermore, the triple use of YHWH in this prayer emphasizes the importance and nature of the prayer. To say something three times in Hebrew was a technique used to solemnize or emphasize something. Hebrew had no word endings for superlatives like English ("the tallest"), so repeating a word three times functions that way: "tall, tall, tall" meant "the tallest". For example, in Isaiah's vision in the Temple (Isaiah 6), he sees creatures flying around the throne of God singing "holy, holy, holy." This was the Hebrew way of saying, "the most holy." Balaam strikes his donkey three times (Num 22). Daniel says his prayers three times a day (Daniel 6). Many sacrifices include three acts. We even see this Hebrew practice make its way into the New Testament: Peter denies Jesus three times, indicating that it was a complete denial (John 18).

Finally, the importance of this prayer is not only in these original elements, but in its constant use throughout Jewish and Christian history. For example, silver amulets or charms engraved with these words were found in a tomb in the Valley of Hinnom outside Jerusalem. These were worn as a necklace or a bracelet, as a reminder of the prayer. Christian inscriptions containing this prayer are found in the city of Thessalonica from around the fifth century AD. The prayer is often used by Christians and Jews today. Most will be familiar with the words, if only from recitation in worship, a book of prayer, or a hymn. The Christian hymn, "The Lord Bless You and Keep You," uses this prayer and is one of the most beautiful in hymnody (both in its lyrical construction and musical composition). When performed well, the seven-fold amen at the end can be a moving benediction for a worship service.

Application

Choose a day this week, and recite this prayer throughout the day for people you encounter. You could also sing the prayer, if you know the hymn. As often as you offer this prayer on that day, recall its ancient beginnings, and its use throughout thousands of years of faith. You are part of a multitude of people, all over the world and throughout time (past, present, and future), who have (or will) recite this prayer in hundreds of different languages on different occasions. You are connected to those people through this prayer-blessing. Focus also on the triple use of the holy name of God. Maybe you can substitute "YHWH" for "Lord," or perhaps you prefer to refrain from speaking that sacred name, reminding yourself of the power and holiness of God as you substitute "Lord" (*adonai*).

Use it as a blessing for fellow Christians, for congregations, and for other groups of people. Use it to bless

The Lord Bless You and Keep You (Num 6.24-26)

your children, your parents, or your spouse at night before sleep. This ancient prayer has a power and a history much like the Lord's Prayer, though many of us rarely use it. Make this prayer a part of your growing arsenal of prayers.

The Song of the Ark
(Num 10.35-36)

"...Arise, O LORD, let your enemies be scattered, and your foes flee before you"

"...Return, O LORD of the ten thousand thousands of Israel."

Background

The Ark of the Covenant was an important artifact and symbol for the Israelites and throughout Jewish and Christian history. The descriptions of its construction are exacting and detailed. It was carried in front of the people of Israel as they wandered the desert. It went before the army in battle. Centuries later, Isaiah had a vision of God sitting on the Ark as His throne. The disappearance of the Ark during the Babylonian exile has resulted in rumors, searches, and even a blockbuster movie, *The Raiders of the Lost Ark*.

Inside the Ark were other key items of Israelite history. Yet they are not just historical, like the Declaration of Independence in Washington D.C., the Crown Jewels in the Tower of London, or the death masks of Roman Emperors in the Berlin Museum. These artifacts were physical representations of God's care and protection of his people. Not only did they remind the Israelites of what God had done in the past, but it was also a reminder that He still was with them.

None of these artifacts exist today, just as many ancient religious objects are lost. The so-called "relics" of Jesus (the grail, a piece of the cross, a few drops of blood, etc.) are probably not authentic, though it is impossible to prove beyond a shadow of a doubt. Nor such things as the other Ark (Noah's), despite the interest and occasional media reports of its discovery. Perhaps God prefers we focus more on faith and action and less on "proof"—just as Jesus pointed out (see Matthew 12.39, 16.4; Luke 11.39; John 20.27).

Meaning

Still, these things were a physical reminder of God's presence for those people. Must we do without the same benefit? Christians found ways to portray physical reminders of the power of God. They build immense and awesome cathedrals to remind us that God is immense and awesome. They make a trek (a pilgrimage) to famous historical locations to emphasize that we walk with God; many fasting or adopt poverty to emphasize sacrifice, or they do something as simple as light candles to depict that "God is light." While not "artifacts," they are physical reminders of spiritual truths.

There are many ways we can mimic the purpose of the Ark, and it may be important to do so as we go about our

The Song of the Ark (Num 10.35-36)

prayer lives. Even small things, such as wearing a cross, using prayer beads, or kneeling when we pray, can add a physical element to our prayers. If we wish to have a vibrant prayer life, it should involve more than just a mental exercise. Some would say that the more senses we use as we talk to God, the more intimate our prayers become.

The prayer in this passage also suggests a practice of prayer that we can use. Notice how, when the Israelites picked up the Ark, they said a prayer asking God for victory. When they brought the Ark back, there was a prayer asking for God to be with them at rest. This prayer, at the beginning and the end, was known as the "Song of the Ark."

The Israelites believed that wherever the Ark was, God was. These beginning and ending prayers appear in the midst of the wanderings in the desert. They had no home and were unsure of their destination. They did not know what the next day might bring. The presence of God was a comfort. It went before them in battle and was believed to give them victory (Joshua 6, 1 Samuel 4–7). Sometimes, a loss in battle was attributed to the Ark being absent (Num 14:44).

The prayers first appear in this passage at the end of a long description of the Israelite's preparation to leave the land (Num 9.1–10.10.35). Those chapters include a description of the first anniversary of the Passover and a description and function of the pillar of fire that led the Israelites by day and the cloud that led them at night. The major themes here are that God will be with His people and that He will give them victory. These ideas are no less important for us than for the Israelites, no less valid for you than they were for Moses.

We can use this prayer as a model for prayer when we begin and end a project or a journey. Note that an important characteristic of the Song of the Ark is that they are the same each time. They are not spontaneous prayers. They are thought-out and precise. We might sometimes criticize the use of "rote" prayers as being impersonal, but they do have a function and are found throughout the Bible. They are particularly useful on more formal occasions—like the beginning and ending of a journey or an event.

Application

You might try writing a "Song of the Ark" of your own, fitting it to the modern world and your circumstances. For instance, you might write one to use before you leave for work or school, and one to pray when you return home. You might write another for the beginning and ending of new projects at work, home, or school. Be creative, make it simple, write it out in your prayer journal and memorize it. Try speaking it for a week and write about your experience.

The Art of Complaining
(Num 11.2)

But the people cried out to Moses; and Moses prayed to the LORD, and the fire abated.

Do you ever complain? Of course you do—we all do. We complain about our life, our surroundings, or the people around us. Complaining is not always bad. In the right amount and done the right way, it can lead us to make positive changes, to adopt a new perspective, or to help us see a problem.

Background

The prayer in Numbers 11.2 is a model of complaining. The previous prayer (Num 10.35–36) described how God would protect his people and help them defeat their enemies. Immediately after, we read that the Israelites are complaining. It must be of the kind we described above—constant and negative—because it makes God angry. He is so angry that he sends fire down to destroy parts of the people's camp. Maybe this was a warning shot, for it does have an effect on the people: they go and complain to Moses! Moses could have then, perhaps, gone to God and complained, but he did not. Instead, he offered a prayer for complainers—an intercession. God listens to Moses and douses the fire. Sadly, this story is the first in a pattern that re-occurs for the next fourteen chapters. The people complain, God sends a warning, they cry to Moses, Moses prays, God relents. At times, even Moses turns to complaining—none of us are above it.

Our reaction to this story might be to criticize the Israelites. What babies! Could they not see how ungratefully they were acting? Before we become self-righteous, however, we should take a good look at ourselves. The biblical story, after all, is not just a story about people long, long ago. It is also a story about us. It tells us what humans are like. What we are like.

Meaning

There are two kinds of people in such stories: those who focus on the problem, and those who focus on the art. Which do you choose to be? The person who complains, or the person who offers prayers for those who complain?

Unfortunately, it is quite easy for complaining to become a hobby. How many of us know someone who makes a practice of complaining? They (or we) may be unaware of just how much they complain. After all, few people admit, "Yes, I am a constant complainer." Because it is hard to see ourselves as others do, it may well be that we are a complainer and do not know it.

The Art of Complaining (Num 11.2)

This is dangerous to our spiritual practices because constant complaining drains the joy from life for us and those around us. More important, it demonstrates a view of the world that is contrary to God's intention. True, we live in a fallen world where sin abounds, and bad things happen. To acknowledge that on occasion is not to be a complainer. But to focus on the fallen aspects and not the remarkable aspects of God's creation is ungrateful and misses the purpose of life.

The Santa Maria delle Grazie church in Milan, Italy, is where Leonardo da Vinci's painting, *The Last Supper*, is located. This renowned work of art was painted about 1498 on a wall of a dining hall in the church. Over the centuries it sustained much wear and tear. It faded, flaked, had a door cut through it, French soldiers scratched out the eyes of the Apostles, and a bomb nearly destroyed the painting during World War II. Restorations took place in the seventeenth, eighteenth, and nineteenth centuries, some of which worsened the damage. The twentieth century saw three attempts. The last was a major restoration that caused much controversy because it made dramatic changes to the colors and shapes. Despite all this, the painting is still one of the most famous in all the world. The style, the textures, and the symbolism have been the subject of constant study by scholars, art aficionados, and the general public for 500 years. No one doubts the skill, the beauty, and the talent of da Vinci. The unique artistic elements and its history have even made it part of many conspiracy theories and rumors in literature and film. Most people have heard of the painting, many have seen pictures of it, but few know of its history or its terrible condition.

Imagine that you are in Italy, standing before this painting. A friend stands beside you. You are face-to-face with one of history's most famous works of art, and you are in awe. Yet all your friend does is discuss the damage, the dirt, the chemical make-up, the mistakes of the restorers, and the loss of the "original." This might be interesting and not entirely incorrect. However, you try to turn the discussion to the art itself: the skill of da Vinci and the beauty of the composition. But it is to no avail—your friend only wishes to discuss the problems. Maybe your friend says, "yes, that is an interesting depiction of John, but the restorers changed the color and shape of John's face." Those critiques, as valid as they might be, stand outside the painting as a creation of art—which is its purpose. Your friend chooses to view what has been done to the painting, rather than what the painting is or what it represents.

To view a painting in this manner might seem silly, but this is what we do with God's creation. We focus on what has happened to the world or what has been done to God's creation, rather than on the work of art created by the Master Creator and its purpose.

Application

This week, do your best to be aware of each time you find yourself criticizing, complaining, or being negative. Stop and make a note of it in your journal. Don't be hard on yourself: just observe. Perhaps you have constructive reasons for complaining. Perhaps you do not do it too often. But you may find you do it more than you thought.

The Art of Complaining (Num 11.2)

If you want to take this exercise to another level of accountability, ask others to catch you at complaining and point it out to you.

At the end of the week, look over your journal and take stock of what you wrote. Were you an aficionado of God's art, or were you a mere fault-finder? Were you one of the complaining masses or were you Moses? Often, the act of admitting our negativity stops us from doing it too often. Take some time to think of ways you can be more appreciative of the Creation today in all its aspects: not just "nature," but people, life, work, and play. Offer a prayer for those who, like you, sometimes adopt complaining as a hobby. Vow to be an "appreciator" of the Art of God rather than a complainer of the problems.

Prayers, Whiners, and Snakes (Num 21.7)

The people came to Moses and said, "We have sinned by speaking against the LORD and against you; pray to the LORD to take away the serpents from us." So Moses prayed for the people.

Background

This brief mention of prayer is one in a series of scenes, some long and some short, which continue to show the complaining nature of the Israelites. In this passage, they leave Mount Hor and take a circuitous route around the land of Edom (perhaps to avoid trouble). The people "become impatient" (literally, in Hebrew, "the soul of the people became impatient/discouraged"). This shows that they are not just experiencing slight irritation—they are irate about their difficulties in the desert. We might be quick to criticize them. After all, God delivered them from slavery, but would we be any better after months or years of wandering in a desert? How chipper would we be when we must wonder where our next camp will be, where the next meal will come from, and if we will find enough water?

The depth and frequency of their complaints is seen by the fact that they are not just criticizing Moses, they are also criticizing God (Num 21.5). They complain about the scarce food and water, and the food they do have they do not like. In the previous prayer, when the people complained like this, God sent fire down to burn parts of the outside of the camp. This time, he sends poisonous snakes which bite some of the people. A few even die.

The people sober up, confess that they have sinned by being ungrateful, and ask Moses to pray for them. Moses offers another intercession and God responds. This time, however, the response is strange. Rather than removing the serpents (as He did with the fire), he tells Moses to make a model of a poisonous serpent and put it up on a tall pole. Whenever a snake bites anyone, they are to look at this totem and they will not die. This seems more like magic or shamanism than any of the previous "miracles" we have read about. While not the norm, there are other instances of this sort of thing in the Bible, where one must do something before being delivered or healed.[1]

Meaning

Why would God answer a prayer by telling someone to perform an act first—especially an action that seems only symbolic? It may be to have the people take part in

---

[1] See, for example, 2 Kings 5.8–14 and John 9.

Prayers, Whiners, and Snakes (Num 21.7)

the deliverance so they could learn, grow, and remember. Perhaps God wanted the people to *act* in some way; to take *some* role in their own healing. Rather than being passive in their deliverance, He wanted them to be active. Most teachers know that active learning works better than passive learning. The lesson about being ungrateful might have a better chance of staying with the people if, having been bit by a snake, they would have to find the bronze serpent and gaze at it.

Or, God may have wanted them to suffer through the situation a bit more. Working through our difficulties (or just surviving them) can make us more mature and stronger. Being bit by snake—but not dying—would make the people stronger in the long run than just taking the snakes away.

Finally, it may just be that God wanted to give them a physical reminder that it is He who cares for them and delivers them. Rather than taking away the snakes, the people had to find the serpent, knowing that the bronze serpent was there at God's command. A reminder that it is He who saves them.

In the Gospel of John, as Jesus speaks to Nicodemus about himself, he refers to this event. "And just as Moses lifted up the serpent in the wilderness, so must the Son of Man be lifted up, that whoever believes in him shall have eternal life."[2] Just as looking to the bronze serpent that God sent saved the people, so looking to Jesus who God sent saves the people. Just as that bronze serpent could help the people learn, grow, and remember, so

---

[2] John 3.14.

looking to Jesus does the same. We learn from him as he teaches us. As we seek him and put his words into practice, we suffer along with him and grow in faith. Jesus and the cross are reminders of God's love for us.

Application

The next time God appears to be ignoring a prayer, it might be worth thinking about this story. Maybe He *has* answered you, but the answer came in the form of something that you need to do. Is there an activity to perform or an action you should take? Perhaps He just wishes you to endure something. Maybe the prayer is being answered in a way to help you to learn, grow, and remember, rather than the problem just being taken away.

Men, Daughters, Wives and Vows
(Num 30)

When a man makes a vow to the LORD, or swears an oath to bind himself by a pledge, he shall not break his word; he shall do according to all that proceeds out of his mouth.

When a woman makes a vow to the LORD, or binds herself by a pledge, while within her father's house, in her youth, and her father hears of her vow or her pledge by which she has bound herself, and says nothing to her; then all her vows shall stand, and any pledge by which she has bound herself shall stand. But if her father expresses disapproval to her at the time that he hears of it, no vow of hers, and no pledge by which she has bound herself, shall stand; and the LORD will forgive her, because her father had expressed to her his disapproval.

If she marries, while obligated by her vows or any thoughtless utterance of her lips by which she has bound herself, and her husband hears of it and says nothing to her at the time that he hears, then her vows shall stand, and her pledges by which she has bound herself shall stand. But if, at the time that her husband hears of it, he expresses disapproval to her, then he shall nullify the vow by which she was obligated, or the thoughtless utterance of her lips, by which she bound herself; and the LORD will forgive her. (But every vow of a widow or of a divorced woman, by which she has bound herself, shall be binding upon her.) And if she made a vow in her husband's house, or bound herself by a pledge with an oath, and her husband heard it and said nothing to her, and did not express disapproval to her, then all her vows shall stand, and any pledge by which she bound herself shall stand. But if her husband nullifies them at the time that he hears them, then whatever proceeds out of her lips concerning her vows, or concerning her pledge of herself, shall not stand. Her husband has nullified them, and the LORD will forgive her. Any vow or any binding oath to deny herself, her husband may allow to stand, or her husband may nullify. But if her husband says nothing to her from day to day, then he validates all her vows, or all her pledges, by which she is obligated; he has validated

Men, Daughters, Wives and Vows (Num 30)

them, because he said nothing to her at the time that he heard of them. But if he nullifies them some time after he has heard of them, then he shall bear her guilt.

Background

The prayer passage for today is different from those we have studied before. First, it consists of a whole chapter which gives instructions about a particular type of prayer—a vow. Second, these instructions are underpinned by some assumptions about gender. This makes it a difficult passage for us to understand because the "rules" are based on ancient views of the roles of men and women, not modern roles—and they are quite different! Those ancient understandings had reasons behind them: they were part of the structure of that society, its economics, and their understanding of nature. We will find some of these aspects strange and perhaps offensive. They seem to flow from a bigoted or misogynistic view of the world. To label this section that way makes it easy to dismiss a complex and complicated set of issues. But such a quick dismissal will also keep us from understanding the passage to its fullest.

Meaning

How ancient people understood the roles of men and women is crucial for making sense of this passage. That world was a lot less safe than ours, especially for women. It was also true that women were usually not as educated as men. Without advancements such as refrigeration and baby formula, women usually had to be at home caring for young children. Because of those realities, society felt that men had the obligation of protecting their daughters and wives. If a daughter lived in the house of her father, he was responsible for protecting her from doing things or saying things that might lead her into danger. When she left home and married, it became the husband's role to protect her. But if she was an orphan or a widow (no father or husband) she was on her own. This is why Jews and Christians were often urged to take care of widows and orphans—there was no state welfare in that world, and a woman could not, with ease, go out and get a job or an education.

In some ways, it seems unfair that the reality of that world prevented women from making their own decisions and acting on their own. On the other hand, it was sometimes the case that the male protector would be punished for illegal or improper acts of the female in his care because society said *he* was responsible.

Understanding these issues makes the rules in this chapter easier to understand (at least from the ancient perspective):

1. If a man makes a vow to God, he is responsible for keeping it.

2. If a daughter, still living at home with her father, makes a vow, then (a) if the father knows about the vow, the daughter is responsible for keeping it; (b) if the father disapproves of it, then she does not have to keep it.

Men, Daughters, Wives and Vows (Num 30)

3. If a woman marries and makes a vow, and (a) her husband knows about it but says nothing, she is responsible for keeping it, but (b) if the husband knows about it and disapproves, she does not have to keep it.

4. If a wife makes a vow, then the same rules apply under #2 above, but it is her husband who can approve or disapprove instead of the father.

5. A widow or divorced woman is responsible for her vows, the same as a man above in #1.

This makes sense from that world view, but it is not how our culture works. What can we learn about prayer vows from those ancient rules? We live in a world where women and men alike can get just about any education or job, and are protected by the same laws and rules. Can we strip away the cultural parts of this passage and apply a timeless principle? Is the principle that vows are to be kept by people who should be responsible for them? (For instance, today, we make similar restrictions on young children and the mentally ill.) Or is it the *practice* that matters, and men are still responsible for approving the vows of their daughters and wives?

Regardless of how you wish to interpret the passage, we can learn some general things about prayer-vows. A vow is part of a prayer made to God, and it is a way of emphasizing the devotion of the one offering it. It somewhat like an oath and somewhat like a bargain. They can be made with rashness (see Jephthah's vow about his daughter in Judges 11.31–32). From this we can stress that, if we offer a prayer-vow, we should consider it in all seriousness. It is not like other prayers that can be offered with spontaneity. If you promise something to God, these passages emphasize that you *must* keep it.

Often, a vow begins with a special time of dedication or abstinence from something (food, wine, sex). Having a special moment as a "kick-off" for the vow, or a physical act, or abstentions are other ways of stressing the importance of promising God that you will do (or not do) something. God keeps his promises with seriousness; He expects the same of us.

Despite the cultural difficulties (and perhaps irrelevancy) of this passage, it does show the emphasis on the importance of keeping vows. Only those who are in positions of weakness or vulnerability are not responsible for their vows—daughters and wives back then, perhaps young children or the mentally ill today.

Application

You might try making a vow in this way—but don't do it rashly. Spend some time and prayer about it; give it a lot of thought. What will you vow to do (or stop doing)? What will you ask God for as part of the vow? Maybe make the first vow for just twenty-four hours or a couple of days. Set a time of prayer and fasting before you begin the vow period to remind yourself of the seriousness of it. Then, in confidence, know also that He will honor your vow, and bless you because of it.

Summary of the Prayers in Numbers

Though there are only five prayers in the book of Numbers, they are varied. Numbers is a book that contains both narrative and legal section (stories and laws), and the prayers reflect that content. There are two intercessions, one blessing, one petition, and a lengthy section on the proper use of vows.

Both intercessions address the complaining of the Israelites (Numbers 11.2; 21.7). God delivered them from slavery and protected them on their desert journey, but they often complained. God warned them by causing fires to break out at the camp perimeter and poisonous snakes to appear. They confessed and asked Moses to pray for them, and God took away the fires—but the complaining continued. The next time, with the snakes, God does not just remove the danger: once bit, they must take action on their own to be saved.

These two prayers teach us four things about the practice of prayer. First, they encourage us to examine ourselves and our attitude towards God. Though we might not intend it, when we complain about life we are criticizing God or, at least, showing impatience with Him. Second, they show that God can send us a warning that we might need to check our attitude. Third, the prayers show that sometimes God thinks we need something more than just a warning. He may wish us to act in some way; to take part in our own growth. Finally, we learn that God sometimes uses suffering to help us grow. Both of these prayers are excellent examples for when we find ourselves caught up in a culture of complaining.

The blessing-prayer in Numbers 6.24–26 is one of the most well-known prayers in the Bible. Moses instructed the priests to pronounce this blessing over all the people before they began their journey: "May the Lord bless you and keep you." Such a practice serves as a reminder that God has adopted us and that He will protect us, bless us, and give us peace. It is a prayer that can be offered for loved ones, for congregations, and for nations.

The petition in Numbers 10.35–26 is a little-known prayer that that reminds us of how we can use prayers of petition in our own lives. This is the Song of the Ark which the Israelites prayed going into battle and when they returned from battle. Prayer framed the time of anxiety and difficulty. Before the battle, the prayer asked for success; after the battle, it asked for God to be with them at rest. We can use the structure of those prayers for our prayers as we begin or end a journey, a project, or anything that encompasses a period of time.

Chapter 27 contains the rules about how ancient Israelites were to use and offer vows, though the passage is influenced by the values of that ancient culture, making it a challenge for us to understand and apply. When we strip away the cultural elements and glean the principles about prayer-vows, we learn that a vow is a way to focus and hold ourselves responsible to God and that we should not offer a vow without serious thought. We also learn that when we keep our vows, God honors us in return.

Summary of the Prayers in Numbers

Just as we saw in Genesis through Leviticus, the prayers in Numbers takes many forms and appears in many different settings. The richness and variety of prayer is found even in this small collection of five prayers. The wide range of styles continues in the book of Deuteronomy.

Deuteronomy

Introduction

The book of Deuteronomy is about looking back and about preparing for a challenging but exciting future. The book begins with a speech by Moses, recounting the difficult history of the Israelites in the desert. Much of the book deals with the law and how the people of God should act, but also warnings and recriminations about the lack of faith. We might expect a lot of petitions and intercessions in such a book, but it is not so.

There are only six prayers. The most common form is a blessing. There are three of them, including a final blessing (a lengthy twelve-part blessing). There is one intercession by Moses for the people; one thanksgiving for the first pickings of the harvest year, and one praise. There are no petitions.

The prayers in Deuteronomy remind us that most of the prayers in the Bible are not petitions or intercessions, even though those are the most common prayers offered in the modern world. There is much more to a life of prayer than just asking for things; our prayers can be rich and varied.

Praying for More
(Deut 1.11)

May the LORD, the God of your ancestors, increase you a thousand times more and bless you, as he has promised you!

Background

The book of Deuteronomy begins with Moses addressing the people of Israel. They stand in the desert of Moab beside a mountain. They had been camping there for some time, waiting at the border of the Promised Land.

Moses reminds them that, when they were staying at Horeb to the south, God had said they had been there long enough. It was time to go to the Promised Land, where He would give them back the land of their ancestors.

Moses told the people that he would not be able to lead them there—they had become so numerous that he was unable to be a judge over so many. He suggested that they appoint leaders from each section and each tribe. They did so, and Israel gained its first structured government. Having taken care of those organizational needs, they set out for the Promised Land. When they arrived, they were afraid of the inhabitants and refused to cross the border.

Moses described their lack of faith and their unwillingness to accept God's offer of new land, protection, and victory. How they had once tried to win the land on their own, without God, and had suffered defeat. Moses continued to describe their history, God's promises, and their failures. Finally, he arrived at the climax of the speech: it is time to enter the Promised Land.

The prayer comes at the beginning of Moses' speech. As he describes that scene back at Horeb, he breaks into a spontaneous blessing. "…at that time I said to you, 'I am unable by myself to bear you.'" Then he gives a reason: God has caused them to multiply so that they were "as numerous as the stars of heaven" (Deut 1.9–10). This is the promise God made to Abraham; that his descendants would be as numerous as the stars of heaven (Exodus 32.13). Moses is affirming that God made a promise, and on that day, as Moses stood looking over the multitude, it was clear that God had kept that promise.

Meaning

Perhaps Moses was overcome at that moment, so moved by the realization of seeing the proof of God's faithfulness. Maybe this is what led him to speak a blessing upon all those faces gazing at him: "May the LORD, the God of your ancestors, increase you a thousand times more and bless you, as he has promised you!"

It is an outburst as if he could not control himself after seeing the evidence of God's faithfulness. Like a husband overcome with love for his wife or a parent for a

Praying for More (Deut 1.11)

child at a particular moment: "I love you so much!" Paul had a similar outburst in Romans 11.33-36 after an extended discussion about God's mercy and mystery; Isaiah's response to his vision of God in the Temple (Isaiah 6) is another example. Peter did the same when he saw the power Jesus had over creation (Luke 5.8).

The last words of Moses' prayer tell us something important as we go about our prayer lives: God is not done yet! Not only did God deliver the Israelites from slavery, deliver them from the Egyptian army, provide them food and water in the desert, multiply them by thousands and thousands, give them victory in battle, and provide them with land of their own—but Moses believed he would do even more: "may the Lord increase you a thousand times more!"

Application

Can we pray like this? If we have been blessed—perhaps with plenty—might it not be selfish and ungrateful to pray for "a thousand times more"? It is important to note the attitude with which the blessing is uttered by Moses. The focus is not on getting something; it is on God's mighty power. He can do things no one expects or thinks possible! With the right attitude, such a prayer can be a wonderful praise of the power and love of God. For example, read this prayer of Paul in Ephesians 3: "Now to him who by the power at work within us can accomplish abundantly far more than all we can ask or imagine, to him be glory in the church and in Christ Jesus to all generations, forever and ever. Amen."

This week, practice praying with such boldness, Not boldness that you will get what you want, but boldness in your trust of just how powerful God is. He is capable of giving even more than we can imagine. Be thankful for what has been before, and be in awe for what God will still do.

Perspective in Fear
(Deut 3.24-25)

"O Lord GOD, you have only begun to show your servant your greatness and your might; what god in heaven or on earth can perform deeds and mighty acts like yours! Let me cross over to see the good land beyond the Jordan, that good hill country and the Lebanon."

I am impressed by people, who, in the midst of tragedy or suffering, can still see the goodness and blessings of God. I do not mean those who are in denial, "Oh, it's not that bad: God is good" or those who have a Pollyanna attitude. Psychologists tell us that to properly deal with a difficult situation, we have to name it for what it is. Perhaps we have all been guilty of telling someone "this is all part of God's plan," or, worse, at the death of a loved one, "God wanted another angel." Tragedy is painful. To pretend otherwise is to deny reality, and denying reality is not a healthy way to deal with pain.

When we suffer, our world tends to close in on us, and we lose perspective. We only see the pain, and so it appears that pain is all there is. This is not reality, and so not the healthiest way to make our way through suffering.

Somewhere between mindless positivism and overwhelming negativism is the proper attitude. There are many examples of this balance in the Bible; biblical characters who were able to keep the negative aspects of their sufferings and the positive aspects of life in perspective. Perhaps it is a combination of faith, God's help, and maturity. Perhaps it is personality and upbringing. It is probably both of those and more. Regardless, this is the attitude to strive for when we are suffering.

Background

The prayer in Deuteronomy 3.24–25 is part of the same passage as the previous prayer we examined in 1.11. It appears in the midst of the speech given by Moses to the people of Israel as they prepare to enter the Promised Land. He has recited the history of the people in the desert, reminding them of the dangers they encountered and how God saved them each time. The first prayer came at the beginning of the speech; this one is in the middle.

Just before the prayer, Moses speaks of various kings who had opposed the people of Israel, and how God brought victory to his own. Now, on the verge of entering the Promised Land, Moses describes how the spoils, lands, and cities were going to be divided among the tribes. He reminds them that God does not want them to be afraid of those they will have to fight to get the land because He with them. It would be understandable if the Israelites were afraid—they were poised to enter a large area of land and conquer the people who lived in it. Those people outnumbered the Israelites by a good

Perspective in Fear (Deut 3.24-25)

amount. They were more experienced in battle, more vicious, and attempting to protect their land. Still, God tells his people not to worry, because, if they follow His instructions, they will be victorious.

Meaning

But which of us would not be worried? Which of us would not be worrying about the coming days, weeks, or months of fighting and loss of life? Yet Moses addresses none of those issues: instead, his prayer is a praise offered to God because He has "only begun to show" His greatness and might. In fact, Moses asks if he can be a part of it. He wants to join the people in their battle.

Many years ago, during my doctoral studies, my wife and I became good friends with my Ph.D. mentor and his wife. About halfway through my dissertation, he was diagnosed with an aggressive form of cancer. We watched the ups and downs, the good news and the bad news, and their struggles with surgery, healing, chemotherapy, and relapses. My wife and I marveled at their ability to name the suffering for the terror that it was, to share the difficulties and the fears, and yet still portray strength through their knowledge that God was sovereign. They did not say, "it's all God's will," but neither did they blame God. They did not say, "Oh, we trust God," but it was clear that they did. They suffered in a quiet and dignified way. They never quit serving others and they did not lose sight of the One who gave them life and promised them eternal life. After he died, his wife continued to be an example for us of strength in suffering, of proper perspective in the midst of real difficulties, while still acknowledging how difficult suffering can be.

Moses was no Pollyanna: he had shown his ability to be afraid, complain, and even lacked faith many times during the forty years in the desert. He was not naive about the forces arrayed against them. Yet, he could also focus on what God was telling them: trust Me. Like my mentors, he did not downplay the fears or the anxieties of the future, but he also kept in mind the fact that there is a larger reality.

In our times of suffering, in the midst of an uncertain and scary future, we should remember to pray in this way—even if we are afraid and unsure. To remember that God stands above it all. Even though there is no guarantee that the pain or suffering will go away, there is something more important than avoiding suffering. It is that God is over all, God loves you, and God's plan works itself out in the long run. In the worst of times, I find this a difficult task. But passages like this, and people like my friends, help me remember, and give me strength. I have found that offering prayers in that manner re-enforce the truth of that for me.

Application

If you are suffering, try praying this prayer of Moses, or share it with someone who might benefit from it. Perhaps you might copy the prayer into your journal to remind you of this lesson when you are suffering or even just anxious about the future. Focus on the God who stands above all reality, and give Him thanks.

Do Not Forget
(Deut 8.10)

You shall eat your fill and bless the LORD your God for the good land that he has given you.

Background

This call to prayer occurs in the midst of a passage that addresses the problem of forgetting the blessings we have. Just before this prayer, the writer repeats the Ten Commandments (Deut 5.1–33), discusses why the Law is so important (6.1–25), and presents the "whats" and "whys" of how Israel was to act towards other nations (7.1–26). The entire passage is structured around two phrases, poetic negatives of each other: "Remember" and "Do not forget." After each is a lengthy list of the things God did for the Israelites, including the provision of manna, clothes, water, food, and protection. We may not often think of the staples of life as blessings, but without food, water, or clothing, we would die within a short time. Whether a family farmed their own food or bought it from someone, its origin was in God. Near the end of the passage, God warns the people: do not think these things come about by your own hand, and, more important, if you forget that it is God who gave them, bad things can happen.

The call to prayer is a simple prayer. It comes in the middle of a discussion of the importance of "remembering" and follows immediately after a description of the land's abundance of food and water. The prayer is like a blessing for a meal: "You shall eat your fill and bless the Lord your God for the good land he has given you."

Despite its simplicity and brevity, this prayer speaks volumes. Enjoy what you have and then offer a blessing to the One who provided it. Do not forget.

Meaning

We are people who sometimes forget a lesson soon after learning it. Whether it is a good or bad event, time tends to diminish our memory of it. We forget the gratitude we felt; we forget the fear we had. As I write this, the United States of America just observed the ten-year anniversary of the September 11 attacks on the World Trade Center, the Pentagon, and the attempted attack on the Capitol Building. When the planes hit those buildings, I was just leaving home to teach a class at a university. I remembered driving to campus and listening, numb, to the news pouring in. I arrived at the classroom to find a room of stunned students who could hardly speak, except to say "Why?" I did not have an answer to that question, except to say that this event, just like many others throughout history, demonstrates that evil exists in our world. Yet God still cares about us, even if terrible events happen

Do Not Forget (Deut 8.10)

and we do not know why. I prayed with them and dismissed the class.

In the following weeks, as I went to and from campus, almost every overpass I drove under had ribbons tied to the fences, signs that read "USA," "United we stand," "we are with you, FDNY," and so on. Many of the bridges had people standing on them, waving flags and chanting as the cars drove underneath. Other demonstrations of unity were everywhere. To most of us, we felt like one people again. We were united in our shared geography, culture, and history. We were united in our resolve not to give in to fear or defeat. As we watched and learned of the heroics of emergency response teams, we had a sense of pride and patriotism that I had not experienced in my life. We had gained a perspective that—despite the differences between groups and individuals—we believed the same on important issues: freedom, heroism, courage, and the ideals of a free society. There was a new civility.

Unfortunately, it was not long before many began to lose that perspective. Within months, some denounced the attack as the fault of the US. Others said the US had been behind the attacks. A couple of professors at my own University objected to a "United We Stand" poster as a partisan political statement rather than a simple declaration of unity in the midst of calamity.

As I write, ten years later, we are as divided as I can ever remember. We are divided on politics, culture, race, class, and so on. Political and social differences are not differing philosophies to be debated and studied, they are vehicles to attack groups and individuals personally. Political and social rhetoric is judgmental and dismissive, with little evidence of any desire for open and engaging debate. Personal attacks and name-calling are the first weapons of choice by politicians. Flash mobs rob local stores. People fight on buses and in McDonald's, every few weeks there is a new group protesting unfairness, injustice, or oppression by someone. There is a different tone in society, and it does not say "united we stand." We are more divided by our disagreements about than united on where we agree.

As Christians, we do the same thing in our relationships with people. We do it in our relationship with God. The good things God and others have done for us fade into time. All the blessings, protections, and favors become less meaningful (many of which we may not have deserved in the first place). Instead, we focus on the difficulties, oppressions, and suffering. In trying times, it is understandable: pain tends to diminish our perspective. Much like a severe cut on your arm—the rest of your healthy body gets ignored.

Application

This week, take some time with to sit down with your prayer journal and think back over the last week. Write down any good things you gained, saw, or experienced. It could be everyday staples: your shelter, your transportation, or your food. It could be relationships: family, friends, or co-workers. Once you have written these down, consider the larger picture of your life: the place you live in, the place in life you occupy now, your education—formal or experiential. The availability of information through books, TV, and the internet. The ease of

Do Not Forget (Deut 8.10)

communication with almost anyone in the world. These are all gifts that God has given you.

After you have made your list and considered the context, offer a brief blessing to God for each one along the model of the prayer above. Eat your fill, and bless God for the good things He has given you.

Extreme Prayer
(Deut 9.26-29)

I prayed to the LORD and said, "Lord GOD, do not destroy the people who are your very own possession, whom you redeemed in your greatness, whom you brought out of Egypt with a mighty hand. Remember your servants, Abraham, Isaac, and Jacob; pay no attention to the stubbornness of this people, their wickedness and their sin, otherwise the land from which you have brought us might say, 'Because the LORD was not able to bring them into the land that he promised them, and because he hated them, he has brought them out to let them die in the wilderness.' For they are the people of your very own possession, whom you brought out by your great power and by your outstretched arm."

Background

This prayer is part of a remembrance of a famous event at Mt. Sinai. It is the story of the golden calf. Moses had ascended the mountain to receive God's guidelines for His people. He was gone longer than the people thought he should be. They become restless and angry and decide that other gods must have been responsible for their deliverance from Egypt. They made idols for these "gods" and began to worship them. God moved to destroy them and start again with Moses and his descendants as the new people of God. Moses begged Him to reconsider. After almost six weeks of prayer, God relented.

Meaning

The context of this passage is the giving of the Law to the people of Israel. It focuses on all that has happened to them and the history of God's acts. Moses reminded them of this event at Mount Sinai and recalled the prayer that he offered for them.

First, Moses says that the people of God have been rebellious the entire time he has known them. If you are familiar with the books of Exodus, Leviticus, and Deuteronomy, you will likely agree. Though they are "God's people," they often rebelled against him, sometimes in offensive ways (such as the golden calf). While it is easy for us to look back at them and judge them with harshness, what if that sort of analysis was turned on us? Could we also be described the same way? Could Moses say us, "you have been rebellious your entire life"? We may not have built golden calves to worship, but we have placed other things at the center and focus of our lives: career, self, money, loved ones, etc. Have we been faithful and subservient, never losing our focus on God?

Extreme Prayer (Deut 9.26-29)

Moses recalls that he "lay prostrate before the Lord" in prayer for forty days and forty nights begging God not to destroy them. This is remarkable. Moses prayed for almost a month and a half! We can assume he stopped to eat and to sleep, but other than that, he spent every moment in prayer. I find my mind drifting from prayer after more than five minutes! Perhaps we need to stretch our ability to pray for lengthy periods of time.

Finally, note that Moses' extreme prayer is not for *himself*; it is on behalf of others. If God came to one of us and said, "I am going to build a new nation around *you*: you shall be the new figurehead of a people," how many of us would say, "no, let's keep working with the current set of ungrateful whiners"? Was this offer difficult for Moses to turn down? He had experienced plenty of frustrations of his own from the people: they had criticized him without mercy, too. Yet he spends forty days and nights praying for these immature and self-centered people. It may tell us something about Moses—but what does it say about the nature of prayer?

With these three elements in mind, try engaging in an extended prayer time for someone else. Choose someone who you believe doesn't deserve it, especially if they have been a bother and a frustration to you. Don't begin by trying to pray for a month and a half. Instead, prayer without a break for ten or twenty minutes—longer than your typical session. The demands of our lives—jobs, children, living spaces—need attention and may make long prayer times difficult. But we should remember that our time with God is just as important as those other things in our lives. Of course, Moses' lengthy prayer was during a severe crisis. The question we should ask ourselves is whether, outside of times of crisis, are we shortchanging our time talking to God?

Application

This week, try an extended time of prayer. Plan it ahead of time. Maybe you will try ten minutes one day, fifteen minutes then next, and so on. Adjust as necessary. Perhaps you can schedule a lengthy session every few days or once a week. Maybe you do longer session only on a weekend day, or on a day off. Decide when and where you will pray, inform your friends and family, shut off your phone and other distractions, and seek to explore what Moses experienced.

A Prayer for First Fruits (Deut 26.13-15)

"I have removed the sacred portion from the house, and I have given it to the Levites, the resident aliens, the orphans, and the widows, in accordance with your entire commandment that you commanded me; I have neither transgressed nor forgotten any of your commandments: I have not eaten of it while in mourning; I have not removed any of it while I was unclean; and I have not offered any of it to the dead. I have obeyed the LORD my God, doing just as you commanded me.

Look down from your holy habitation, from heaven, and bless your people Israel and the ground that you have given us, as you swore to our ancestors—a land flowing with milk and honey."

Many of us have grown up in a world typified by industry—the Industrial Age. Most would say that we have moved beyond that into a world that is post-industrial and now revolves around information: we are in the Information Age. That culture affects how we read, hear, and think. We view life and philosophy (and religion!) through the lens of an Industrialist-Informationist. It is our worldview.

When we read Scripture, we should remind ourselves that the people who wrote and lived in those stories were part of a pre-industrial age. Their world revolved around agriculture. So it is not surprising that many of the ceremonies, prayers, and religious instructions found in Scripture revolve around the agricultural year. Had the Bible been written in the 20th or 21st century, the prayers would have a different cycle and setting.

Background

This prayer is part of the instructions about offering "first fruits" to God. It is connected preparing, planting, and reaping crops. While few of us today spend little or no time performing such tasks, the principle of "first fruits" is timeless and can still apply.

The concept is this: the people worked hard to prepare the soil, to plant seeds, and to tend the crops by watering, weeding, and pruning. Considerable attention was paid to the weather, waiting for the first sprouts to appear, and to the animal and insect life in and around the fields. This was done to produce a good crop, so that, in turn, when the harvest came, there would be healthy, fresh, and abundant food to provide to the families and the rest of society. When the first crop was ready for harvesting, the people could look at the fruit, vegetables, or grain, to know how the rest of the harvesting season would turn out. If the production were full and rich, it would be a good year. If it were small and sparse, it would be a thin

A Prayer for First Fruits (Deut 26.13-15)

year. For the Israelites, no matter the result, the mystery and awe of creation was evident. Through their efforts, combined with God's creation of the process of biology, magic happens. From a seed comes food and drink that sustains life, provides meals for social occasions, and provides part of the economy of buying and selling that drove society. This all came from God's power of creation: "Let there be!"

This is where the practice of offering thanks for the "first fruits" comes from, and it emphasizes that it is God who caused the results. Once a farmer had examined those first few mature fruits, vegetables, or grains, it was time to give God thanks because, no matter how much we worked for it, it was His power that enabled any of it to happen at all. He is the genesis and the nurturer of everything that sits on our plates and fills our cups. To them, it was right to give thanks and to offer some of the "first fruit" back to God, because He has blessed them and sacrificed for them. So they sacrificed a bit of what they had, giving back to him in thanksgiving and gratitude.

Meaning

Today, we can do the same even though the context and work we do is in an office, a service job, or in and about the home. We prepare through education and experience, we tend and nurture our skills, we do what needs to be done for our job, family, and society. For most of us, the "first fruits" are not the first apples or corn of the season. It may be the end of a product development, it may be tax time, it may be the end of a school year. But at some point, the results of our preparation and maintenance comes to fruition (note the root of that word "fruit"). While we often cannot give back to God the physical results of our work, we can still sacrifice by offering some of our paycheck (which is one result of our work) to a church, a charity, or some other organization that does the work of God. We can also offer our time or skills to support the work of God.

At "first fruits," the harvesters brought the produce to town, and the whole village knew what the rest of the year would bring. It was a time for great rejoicing—or a thanksgiving for a little in spite of inclement weather. Trying times can also form part of the offering of the "first fruits." In an agricultural society, there could be drought, disease, or storms. Disasters and thin years take place in a modern society, too, but the difficulties might be economic problems, job layoffs, unanticipated medical expenses, and so on. So, while we do our best, we do not always know what the coming year holds. That does not negate the fact that God is in control and that it is His power that sustains us in the good times and the difficult times. So, regardless of the type of "harvest," it is right to give thanks to God and to ask for His continued care. After all, if He chose to withdraw from the universe, to stop empowering nature and the environment, we would all suffer and die in a short time.

The practice of "first fruits" is, then, another way in prayer to remind us of the power of God and His intimate connection with every part of the world. We may not always understand why we have abundant years and then scarce years, but both are evidence of God's work in the world. As the Creator and Sustainer, the end of each time

A Prayer for First Fruits (Deut 26.13-15)

period, of each project, and of each set of tasks is a time that we can use to connect to God in prayer.

Application

Write in your journal today some of the moments during projects, time periods, or milestones and guideposts that might be your modern equivalent of a first harvest. How does it tell you how the future will turn out? How can you celebrate it or use it as a reminder of God's power in your life? How can you use the results to give back to God in some way? Mark these dates on your calendar during the year as your special "first fruits" celebration. Plan a time of prayer and thanksgiving for those days.

Four Kinds of Blessings
(Deut 33.6-29)

May Reuben live, and not die out,
  even though his numbers are few.
And this he said of Judah:
  O LORD, give heed to Judah,
  and bring him to his people;
  strengthen his hands for him,
  and be a help against his adversaries.
And of Levi he said:
  Give to Levi your Thummim,
  and your Urim to your loyal one,
  whom you tested at Massah,
  with whom you contended at the waters of Meribah;
  who said of his father and mother,
  "I regard them not";
  he ignored his kin,
  and did not acknowledge his children.
  For they observed your word,
          and kept your covenant.
  They teach Jacob your ordinances,
          and Israel your law;
  they place incense before you,
  and whole burnt offerings on your altar.
  Bless, O LORD, his substance,

and accept the work of his hands;
crush the loins of his adversaries,
of those that hate him, so that they do not rise again.
Of Benjamin he said:
The beloved of the LORD rests in safety—
the High God surrounds him all day long—
the beloved rests between his shoulders.
And of Joseph he said:
Blessed by the LORD be his land,
with the choice gifts of heaven above,
and of the deep that lies beneath;
with the choice fruits of the sun,
and the rich yield of the months;
with the finest produce of the ancient mountains,
and the abundance of the everlasting hills;
with the choice gifts of the earth and its fullness,
and the favor of the one who dwells on Sinai.
Let these come on the head of Joseph,
on the brow of the prince among his brothers.
A firstborn bull—majesty is his!
His horns are the horns of a wild ox;
with them he gores the peoples,
driving them to the ends of the earth;
such are the myriads of Ephraim,
such the thousands of Manasseh.
And of Zebulun he said:

Four Kinds of Blessings (Deut 33.6-29)

Rejoice, Zebulun, in your going out;
    and Issachar, in your tents.
They call peoples to the mountain;
there they offer the right sacrifices;
for they suck the affluence of the seas
and the hidden treasures of the sand.
And of Gad he said:
  Blessed be the enlargement of Gad!
    Gad lives like a lion;
    he tears at arm and scalp.
  He chose the best for himself,
  for there a commander's allotment was
        reserved;
  he came at the head of the people,
  he executed the justice of the LORD,
    and his ordinances for Israel.
And of Dan he said:
  Dan is a lion's whelp
    that leaps forth from Bashan.
And of Naphtali he said:
  O Naphtali, sated with favor,
    full of the blessing of the LORD,
    possess the west and the south.
And of Asher he said:
  Most blessed of sons be Asher;
  may he be the favorite of his brothers,
    and may he dip his foot in oil.
  Your bars are iron and bronze;
  and as your days, so is your strength.
There is none like God, O Jeshurun,
who rides through the heavens to your help,
    majestic through the skies.
  He subdues the ancient gods,

shatters the forces of old;
he drove out the enemy before you,
and said, "Destroy!"
So Israel lives in safety,
untroubled is Jacob's abode
in a land of grain and wine,
where the heavens drop down dew.
Happy are you, O Israel! Who is like you,
a people saved by the LORD,
the shield of your help,
and the sword of your triumph!
Your enemies shall come fawning to you,
and you shall tread on their backs.

Background

The last prayer in the book of Deuteronomy is a blessing—actually a series of blessings—given by Moses upon the tribes of Israel. The blessings are specific to these ancient tribes, so it might seem there is not much for us to learn about our own prayer-blessings. But a little understanding about the geographic and historical context of these tribes presents some key insights about blessing-prayers.

The passage begins with a brief summary of what the Israelites have been through since they left Egypt (33.2–5).[1] After the summary, the blessings follow one after the

---

[1] It is strange here that Moses is mentioned in the third person, as if he is not the one offering the prayer. Perhaps a later writer

Four Kinds of Blessings (Deut 33.6-29)

other for each tribe.[2] As noted above, many the blessings merely ask that the tribe survive. The blessing of Reuben (32.6) takes its form because the tribe had lost many of its members and was in danger of extinction. Likewise, the second blessing, on Judah (32.7) asks for continued strength against enemies. So, a blessing can request a status quo—even the bare minimum—depending on the circumstances.

The third blessing might baffle us a bit because it asks that God give to the tribe of Levi his "Thummim" and "Urim" (32.8–11). The men of the tribe of Levi were the priests of Israel. The "Thummim" and "Urim" were colored stones, like dice, used by the priests to determine God's directions to the people of Israel.[3] This blessing is asking God to assist Levi as the tribe carries out its duties, just as we could pray blessings upon others as they perform their duties.

The next two blessings (32.12, 32.13–17) do not ask for anything, but only affirm blessings already enjoyed. Benjamin is God's "beloved" (much like Benjamin was the favorite son of Jacob) and that God "rests between

---

added this later. Maybe this is an example for us that, if a blessing is to be given in public before a large number of people (as this one is) it is helpful to "set the stage" with a brief introduction.

[2] Note that there are not twelve tribes, but eleven. This is because the tribe of Simeon was absorbed by the tribe of Judah in the early period after Israel took occupation of Canaan.

[3] See also 1 Sam 10.22, 14.41, 22.10–16, 28.6; 2 Sam 5.19–23, 21.1, and 1 Kings 1.17–48. I will discuss the practice of "casting lots" in these passages in the next volume, *Praying Through the Bible, Volume 2 (Judges–2 Samuel)*

his shoulders." The latter is a reference to Jerusalem, the city of God because it was in the middle of the land of the tribe of Benjamin. The next blessing (to Joseph) is poetic and focuses a good bit of its imagery on creation: land, fruit and produce, and the water from below. This is because the land of Joseph's tribe was in some of the most fertile lands in Israel. The end of the prayer mentions Manasseh and Ephraim, two sons of Joseph, which later became two tribes in place of the tribe of Joseph, which brings the number of tribes back to twelve after the loss of the tribe of Simeon.

The next two tribes receive brief blessings in two parts. Both are affirmations of existing blessings because the tribes of Zebulun and Issachar were beside the sea, from which they had many blessings from fishing and trade (32.18–19).

Gad's blessing (32.20–21) is another prayer that emphasizes existing blessings. The tribe of Gad lived in some of the best lands. Additionally, the tribe showed great strength in the battle for the land against the Canaanites.

The tribe of Dan is blessed with a hope or prophecy of the future, or at least portends the potential. Poetic language likens Dan to lion cub that will leap forth with energy and strength (32.22).

Naphtali's blessing is also related to its current blessings, and to the land that tribe inhabited (32.23). Part of this land was along the north shoreline of the Sea of Galilee, a fertile area for crops and fishing.

Finally, a more traditional blessing (using the words "may he...") is pronounced upon the tribe of Asher (32.24-25). The prayer asks that Asher be blessed, that the tribe be a favorite among all the tribes, and that "he dip his foot in oil." This refers to olive oil, used for many things in the ancient world, including the act of anointing someone for a special status or a task. Bathing your feet in it would be a sign of extravagance.[4]

Meaning

We might think that a blessing is always a prayer in which we ask God to give something to another person. The passage here shows that a prayer-blessing can be more than that. First, a blessing can acknowledge a gift of God that has already been given. In this way, it serves as an affirmation of what God has done and implies a thanksgiving. Second, a prayer-blessing does not have to ask for some great gift or enlargement. It can just ask that God give a person strength or just to help them survive. Third, a blessing can ask God to assist someone in their duty, role, or path. The overlap with thanksgiving and petition is strong, but note that the prayer is couched as a blessing, uses the language of blessing, and is focused on what God will do.

---

[4] The name "Jeshurun" used in the blessing another name for Israel.

Application

So, these blessings, rooted as they are in their circumstances, can be used as models to enrich our prayer-blessings. Try using each of the types. Choose four people to offer blessings upon today. For one, pray for strength and survival, rather than gifts or boons (see 32.6, 7). For another, pray a blessing that emphasizes their current conditions (see 32.12, 13–17, 18–19, 20-21, 22-23) as a confirmation of God's goodness. For the third, pray a blessing that asks God to assist someone in their work, like the blessing upon Levi (32.8–11). Finally, for the fourth, offer a traditional blessing that asks for gifts to be given in the future (32.24-25).

Summary of the Prayers in Deuteronomy

There are six prayer passages in the book of Deuteronomy. At the beginning of the book, Moses stands before a new generation of Israelites: those who will finally enter the Promised Land. He recounts what happened during the decades in the desert: the struggles, sufferings, wars, and betrayals. It is not all negative; some of the ways God protected them is also mentioned. But most of the speech serves as a warning to the people who are preparing to enter the Canaan and will have to fight for the land. In a book such as this, we might expect a lot of prayers of intercession and petition. Yet Deuteronomy contains only one intercession and no petitions; and there are three blessings (the last of which is made up of twelve blessings), an intercession, a praise, and a thanksgiving.

We have noted that, at least in modern times, our prayers tend to be heavy on asking and begging and light on praise and blessing. When we seek something for ourselves or others, we ask for things. When we suffer, or when we see others suffering, we ask for help. There is nothing wrong with this, of course. Asking for things from God is encouraged throughout the Bible. Yet if our primary types of prayers are petition and intercession, while the major types in the Bible are praise, thanksgiving, and blessing, this might be a sign that we are focusing too much on ourselves. We stress how *we* relate to God, but most biblical prayers focus *first* on God and how *He* relates to them.

The first two prayers appear during Moses' speech to the people as they prepare to enter the Promised Land (1.11; 3.24–25). The first is a blessing; the second is a praise. These prayers teach us that our prayers can be offered with boldness because we trust in God's power. We can even do so in the midst of an uncertain and scary future.

The third prayer is another blessing. It reminds us to remember the everyday things of life as blessings (8.10). The next prayer is an intercession by Moses (9.26–29) and an example of prayer in an extreme times. It is prayer as a marathon. This is followed by a thanksgiving for "first fruits" (26.13-15), thanking God for the first crop of the harvest year. It reminds us of how God is connected to us in every part of our lives, in the good and bad, and we can use those times as reminders to thank him for all things.

The final prayer is a twelve-fold blessing pronounced by Moses upon the twelve tribes (33.2–29). Here, we find four types of blessings: a blessing of strength and survival, a blessing of the "now," a blessing for help in one's work, and a more traditional blessing of a gift. These twelve blessings are an example of how rich and varied blessings can be, and how a blessing can overlap with other types of prayer.

Though the number of prayers in Deuteronomy is few, the variety, as in the other books we have examined, is rich. Not only are there prayers that can take many forms (intercession, blessings, praise, etc.), but even within

Summary of the Prayers in Deuteronomy

those forms there can be variety (the four kinds of blessings).

Joshua

Introduction

The book of Joshua is interesting because of its presentation of opposing themes. On the one hand, the story demonstrates God's faithfulness to His people. He had promised them their own land, and in the book of Joshua, He gives it to them. On the other hand, the book full of instances where the people ignored God's directions, acted with greed, and relied on themselves rather than God.

These themes are reflected in the prayers in the book, though there are few. In fact, God speaks to Joshua and others more often than they speak to him![1] God is often angry at his people in these stories. Perhaps the key passage about prayer is not a prayer at all, but a mention of *no* prayer: "So the leaders partook of their provisions, and did not ask direction from the LORD" (9.14). It is clear from following events that they should have prayed and sought guidance from God.

There are eight prayers in the book of Joshua. There are two blessings, but they are brief, and the content is

---

[1] See the frequent refrain "and God said to Joshua" in 1.1; 3.7; 4.1, 4.15; 5.2; 7.10; 8.1, 18; 10.10; 11.6; 13.1; 30.1. See also 5.6.

unknown: "Joshua blessed him/them." There is one intercession, one curse, one lament, a confession, a vow, and a petition. (One might even question whether the confession is really a prayer of confession: a man is asked to confess to God, yet he does not offer a prayer, he just admits what he did). Though every prayer type is found in the book of Joshua, each is short and shallow. We are rarely told what the person *said* in the prayer.

All of this fits the purpose of the book of Joshua. God kept His promises, but the people were often selfish and sinful. They ignored God. What can we learn about prayer from such a book? The lessons are all negative. The book of Joshua, more often than not, teaches us what to *avoid* doing.

The book is in six sections: the Israelites enter into the land of Canaan (1.1–5.12), the wars against the people of Canaan (5.13–11.23), the division of the land among the Israelite tribes (12.1–19.15), a call to keep the law as handed down by Moses (20.1–21.45), a threat of a civil war (22.1–34), and a conclusion which comes at the end of Joshua's life (23.1–24.33). Most of the prayers occur in the sections about the wars and the civil war.

The paucity and shallowness of the prayers does not mean that they are not sincere. Most seem to be so. Yet those praying appear distracted as if they are too busy to spend much time in prayer. Or perhaps the author of the book did not think prayer was important to his story. Yet the next book, the book of Judges, is filled with the kinds of prayers found in the other books we have studied. Joshua stands apart when it comes to prayer, and this is likely no accident. Most scholars believe that Joshua and Judges were written by the same person, or at least compiled and edited by the same person. This, along with the

Introduction

fact that God speaks to people in Joshua more often than they speak to him, indicates that the author may be trying teaching us something about prayer: treat it lightly at your own peril!

A Not-Prayer (Joshua 1.17)

Only, may the LORD your God be with you, as he was with Moses.

Background

The book of Joshua begins with God telling Joshua that it is time to lead the Israelites into the Promised Land. God says that He will be with him, just as He was with Moses. Finally, God encourages him to keep the law of Moses and to be courageous.

Joshua immediately tells his commanders to go throughout the camp, announcing to the people that they would set out in three days. It was time to go back to the land of their ancestors.

In response, the people deliver a message for Joshua that they will obey him, just as they did Moses, and they will go where he tells them. Then, they say this: "Only, may the LORD your God be with you, as he was with Moses."

Is this a prayer? It sounds a bit like a blessing, or perhaps an intercession, yet it has an off-handedness about it. It is as if they are focusing more on Joshua, themselves, and the past, rather than offering a prayer for Joshua.

The command of Joshua and the response of the people is best understood as an exchange of oaths between a new leader and his people. This was a common practice in the ancient world. The contents are what anyone of that age would expect. Perhaps this explains why the "prayer" seems a bit distant.

Meaning

I have included the passage in our study as if the people *are* asking God to be with Joshua. Yet it may not be a prayer; it could be that the people are only be placing a limit on their loyalty to Joshua. After all, the entire first chapter emphasizes that Joshua is the new leader and successor to Moses. God says it; Joshua acts on it; the people affirm it and declare their loyalty. So the words above may be a way of saying, "you have our loyalty, but *only as long as God is with you*." In other words, they are not asking God to be with Joshua; they are placing a condition on how far their commitment to him will go.

If it is a prayer, then it is a simple petition. We have seen a few of these throughout our study. Yet the language here is different—it is not particularly poetic, spiritual, or moving. If it is a prayer, it is rather off-handedly inserted in the middle of a response that has little to say to God or about God. As we noted in the introduction to Joshua, this attitude is prevalent in the book: the few prayers are almost like brief asides.

A Not-Prayer (Joshua 1.17)

It is more likely, I think, that this is not a prayer. If so, we might ask, "why is there no prayer?" These are the people of God, not just any nation of people. Why is there no full prayer at the beginning of the new leader's term, or at the start of an offensive to take the land back? Why is there no petition for God to be with Joshua and the people? Why is there no thanksgiving for bringing them safe to this moment? When Moses began to lead the people, the people had prayed to God for a leader (Exodus 2.23). Moses prayed for the leader of the Egyptians during the Plague episodes (Exodus 9.28–29, 33, and 10.17-18). When the people were delivered from the Egyptians, all the men offer a prayer of praise (15.1-18), and the women did the same (15.21). Finally, whenever the people moved out of camp in the desert (behind the ark of the covenant), a prayer was offered (Num 10.25–36).

Why is it, then, at this critical moment in Israel's history, there is no real prayer? What can we learn about prayer from the lack of prayer?

We are busy people. Even those who do not have a typical "nine-to-five" job are busy. Those who have worked long and hard all their life and are retired are often busy. Rarely does anyone say, "Oh, I am not too busy these days." Sometimes, we will even say we are busy when we are not. It is as if we measure value by how busy we are.

The problem with that, of course, is that "busyness" can distract us from more important things. When Jesus visited the house of Martha and Mary, Martha busied herself in the kitchen while her sister sat listening to Jesus. When Martha complained that she was doing all the work, Jesus said, "Martha, Martha, you are worried and distracted by many things; there is need of only one thing. Mary has chosen the better part…" (Luke 10.38–42). It is not that being a good host is unimportant. It was perhaps more important in that culture than ours! It was that there was something more important at that moment. A song by Harry Chapin from 1974, entitled "The Cat's in the Cradle," captures this idea. A dad, so busy with work and with providing for his family, has little time for his son. It is not that he does not talk to his son or does not love him. It is quite clear from the lyrics that he cares for his son—but he is so busy providing for his family that he has no time to spend with him. Throughout his son's life, he tells him that they will get around to it, and "you know we'll have a good time then, son." The final verse of the song depicts his son as an older teenager and then as an adult. He loves his dad and talks with him, but is so busy he has no time to spend with his dad—but they will, someday, and "you know we'll have a good time then, dad."

Were the Israelites and Joshua so busy with new leadership, preparing for a new future, preparing for movement and battle, that they had little time for God? Perhaps this is the lesson we can draw from this passage. Are we too busy to offer prayers? At critical moments in life, while we are frantic in preparation, do we forget to pray? Or do we say we'll get around to it when we are less busy? Are we so worried and distracted by many things when there is a need for something else: a blessing, a petition, or an intercession?

A Not-Prayer (Joshua 1.17)

Application

This week, take a quiet moment to recall some times where you have felt too busy to offer an appropriate prayer. Maybe that time is now. Then, consider an upcoming event where a prayer beforehand would be proper. Commit to doing just that, and find a way to remind yourself when the time comes.

A Curse-Prayer (Joshua 6.26)

Cursed before the LORD be anyone who tries to build this city—this Jericho!

At the cost of his firstborn he shall lay its foundation, and at the cost of his youngest he shall set up its gates![1]

Background

If the last passage we examined (Joshua 1.17) was not a prayer, then the first prayer in the book of Joshua does

---

[1] The Septuagint (LXX), a Greek translation of the Hebrew scriptures from a century or so before the time of Jesus, adds a couple of sentences to verse 26 stating that the curse was fulfilled later, when, during the time of King Ahab, someone tried to refortify Jericho, and his son lost his life (it is unclear whether he was offered as a child sacrifice or if he was killed some other way). Whoever added this passage took it from 1 Kings 16.34. (There apparently were people who lived in the city later without being punished, but they did not re-fortify it. See Josh 18.21, Judg 3.13, and 2 Sam 10.5).

not appear until here in 6.26. Many important events have come and gone, with no mention of prayer. Joshua sent spies into the promised land, who find refuge with a prostitute who knows they are from God and will conquer the city. They return to Joshua with a report. No prayers are offered before, during, or after the mission.

The Israelites then strike camp and cross a river, able to do so because God stops it from flowing. No prayers are offered before the crossing, and there are no prayers of praise or thanksgiving after. It is the priests, however, who lead the way across the river and into the promised land, carrying the ark of the covenant. Many commentators have viewed this as a sign of the Israelites' dependence on God. In the context of the whole book, however, it may be that the Israelites saw the ark more as a powerful weapon than a sign of their dependence on God.

When the kings of the land see that miracle and the army of the Israelites, they are afraid. The Israelites celebrate a Passover as a symbolic end of the time between the first Passover in Egypt and this entry into the promised land. Still, there are no prayers.

The large army approaches Jericho, and an angel appears to Joshua, giving him instructions from God. Still, there are no prayers offered. Seven times a day for seven days, the army marches around the city walls, with the priests in front carrying the ark. Again, no prayers. The walls fall, the Israelites kill all the men and women and animals, and rescue the prostitute and her family, just as the spies had promised her (in return for her help).

We then arrive at the first prayer in Joshua. Having explored the prayers in Genesis, Exodus, Leviticus, Numbers, and Deuteronomy, we would expect a prayer of praise, thanksgiving, or blessing for the victory. Instead,

A Curse-Prayer (Joshua 6.26)

we find a curse-prayer. Joshua asks that God curse anyone who ever tries to refortify the city.

Meaning

Is the lack of prayer up to this point, and then the curse-prayer, intended to tell us that they did not pray? Perhaps there were prayers, but the writer did not think it was important to include it. More likely, the writer is telling us something else. Despite all the priestly activity and the appearances of God, these people focus only on their own gains. They see God as a power they can wield rather than a God they should follow with humility.

It is true that Joshua is a different kind of literature than the previous five books, and it is of a kind that makes most modern people uncomfortable. It deals with a war authorized by God. It involves the killing of women, children, and animals, and the destruction of towns. Some commentators address this by saying that God never intended that level of brutality. This was only the Israelites being overzealous. While sometimes that appears to be true, it is clear that God *did* order many of the actions. The purpose is that there be no trace of the pagan culture left that might later influence the Israelites.

As difficult as this might be to accept, we cannot change what the text says in an attempt to rescue God from something that offends modern minds. He did order such brutality. At the same time, the Israelites did not always do as He asked, and, at other times, they went far beyond God's orders. What are we to make of it all? We do not have space here to deal with these difficult theological and historical-cultural issues. We can note that

Joshua is not just a history of events, like a textbook or a record book. Joshua is a *theological* history. It is meant to tell us something about God, people, and societies. It is also important to remember that the ancient culture of the Near East had a different view of war, honor, religion, and death than modern Western cultures.

Despite those difficulties, we can learn something about prayer from these passages. This prayer is a prayer that asks God to curse people. We have encountered four curse-prayers before, all in Genesis (9.25–27; 27.12–13; 29, 39–40). Each of those was connected with a blessing: if you do this, then a blessing will come; if not, then a curse will come. Joshua's prayer, however, contains no blessing.

Solitary curse-prayers are rare in the Old and New Testament. This prayer, like the rest of Joshua, appears to be a reflection of a lack of faith and a focus on self and personal gain. Yet negative lessons about prayer can be as helpful as positive lessons.

First, the act of praying does not necessarily mean that the prayers are sincere, or that the motive behind them is proper. Our prayers can be selfish. We might offer them only out of habit without any real thought or feeling. Our underlying attitude towards God and his creations may be less than noble and sincere in many ways.

Second, our questionable motives in prayer could act as a negative model for others. A cursory reading of Joshua might lead one to think that these are faithful people, following the direction of God and experiencing victories. Yet when we read with care, we see that the stories are examples of God keeping his promises while the people are self-centered. We can be guilty of the same. To others, we might seem to be in God's light and doing

A Curse-Prayer (Joshua 6.26)

well—but in our spirit we are impoverished. Our "success" is due to God's faithfulness, not ours.

Application

This week, spend some time thinking about the prayers you offer. In general, what are your motives and attitude? Are you focused primarily on yourself and your personal gain? Are your prayers rote reputations? Or do you have a genuine concern for others and a sincere attitude? Do you spend time praising God and asking for His will to be done?

Then, spend some time thinking about how others might perceive your life of faith. Would they gain one impression from a cursory examination of your life, and a different impression from a deeper analysis? If you need to change anything about this, what steps could you take?

A Lament
(Joshua 7.7–9)

"Ah, Lord GOD! Why have you brought this people across the Jordan at all, to hand us over to the Amorites so as to destroy us? Would that we had been content to settle beyond the Jordan! O Lord, what can I say, now that Israel has turned their backs to their enemies! The Canaanites and all the inhabitants of the land will hear of it, and surround us, and cut off our name from the earth. Then what will you do for your great name?"

Background

In their battle to take the Promised Land, God instructed the Israelites to destroy certain things completely. This was called *herem*, meaning "devoted thing." In the context of Joshua, this means "a thing devoted to destruction." The language comes from the practice of sacrifice. Sometimes, part of a sacrifice offered to God could be kept by the priests for their own use, such as meat, olive oil, or grain. The rest was burned as an offering to God.

The latter part of the sacrifice was called the *herem*, the "devoted thing."

In the book of Joshua, this concept is applied to the spoils of battle. Because the land was given to Abraham by God, lost, and then to be restored, the battle for it was a holy act, commanded by God. Because there was theological meaning to the battle and the land, some things in it had to be utterly destroyed, that is, completely offered to God. This sometimes included men, women, children, animals, and goods. Many commentators explain these troubling commands to destroy everything as a warning to those to oppose God, and because if they remained, they might tempt God's people into materialism, corruption, or idolatry. For many, this makes the practice no less disturbing. Maybe it just a mystery of God, and we take on faith that this was what God required in those circumstances, which were unique to that time and place.

This story, which includes the prayer above, begins in much the same way as the victory at Jericho. Joshua sent men to spy, they return with information about the enemy, and the army attacks. This time, however, it is the Israelites who lose. This time, it is not a God-believing pagan prostitute who becomes an important character in the story, but a self-centered Israelite clan leader. This time, it is not the faithful non-Israelite and her family who are saved, it is a faithless Israelite family who is condemned.

After the loss, Joshua and the elders are devastated and confused. They fall on their faces before the Ark of the Covenant. They put dust on their heads. Joshua tears his

A Lament (Joshua 7.7–9)

clothes. These three actions are traditional acts of mourning and expressing humiliation. Joshua then offers the prayer above and waits for God's answer.

He responds with anger. He tells Joshua to get up and says that his people have not been faithful. Someone kept some of the spoils of war against God's explicit command. Because of that, the army cannot be victorious because *they* have become the *herem*—the thing destined for destruction. Joshua investigates and discovers that a man named Achan is the one who broke the promise made to God and kept some of the spoils from Jericho.

Why did the Joshua and the Israelites not know about Achan's transgression *before* the battle? Did Joshua, as the leader, not pray to God before he sent in the spies? Did he not seek God's blessing or instructions before he sent in the army? It would seem not. Joshua and his people charged in, so confident of their own power because "God was on their side."

Joshua's prayer is a lament, like others found in the Bible.[1] It begins with a heartfelt cry to God, asking "why?" It describes the reason for the lament (the loss of the battle) and then closes with a reminder to God that, because of what has happened, other people will mock God as powerless.[2] Joshua (and presumably the rest of

---

[1] The only other lament in this volume is Hagar's lament in Gen 21.16, but there are many more throughout the Old and New Testament. See the following footnote for some Psalms of lament; the entire book of Lamentations is, not surprisingly, a lament.

[2] See, for example, Pss 74.10, 18; 79.9; 83.4, 16, 18; Ps 106.8; 109.21; 143.11.

the Israelites) believed that if they lost a battle, it must also mean that God lost a battle. Perhaps *other* nations might think God weak, but God's people should have no concern for that. Instead, they should be asking, "Why did this loss happen? What have we done wrong?"

There are some differences between this lament and most other biblical laments. Most laments look to a future hope in spite of the circumstances; this one is only concerned with the tragedy and the loss. Most laments contain a confession of trust, something like, "I don't understand this situation, but I trust in you, God." Joshua offers no such acknowledgment. In fact, while most laments lead to God revealing some hope for the future or a revelation of salvation, this one written using the language of a lawsuit. Joshua brings his complaint to God and argues his case. God, as the defendant, pleads his side, and the evidence is with Him. Judgment is given. The verdict (and result) is that Israel can only be restored by excising the sinful parts: Achan, his clan, and his belongings must become *herem*.

Meaning

What do we learn about prayer from this lament? Laments have a place in the prayer life of a Christians, though most of us are not likely to offer them often, if at all. As this story demonstrates, our attitude behind a lament is important. We cry out God because of a significant loss, or frustration, or fear. It asks of God, "why did you let this happen?" This is where we need to take care in how we understand laments. Many biblical writers question God's actions (or lack thereof)—sometimes

A Lament (Joshua 7.7–9)

with vehemence. There is a difference between *losing faith* in God's power over events and expressing frustration and confusion with His actions. Even anger towards God is permissible, as demonstrated by some of the Psalms and prophetic books. But even the most critical of laments wind back to a confession of the offerer's limited understanding and expresses trust in God in spite of the circumstances. Joshua's lament is a proper one, as far as it goes, but it does not lead to humility. An arrogance had crept into the Israelites' attitudes. "God is with us" had come to mean, "we cannot lose." They had forgotten that it is only by the grace and gift of God that He was with them—not because of any great work or value of their own.

Most laments, including this one, are offered in public. I cannot recall ever hearing a public lament unless it was a reading of biblical lament. If we do offer laments, it is likely in private. Is there a place in the modern world for the public offering of laments in the community of God?

Application

Consider your attitude as a believer and follower of God. Is there a danger of arrogance because you *are* a follower of God? Do you look down your nose at non-believers (or weak believers)? Good cheer at being "one of God's people" can lead to thinking we are better than others. Examine your attitudes and your prayer life—especially when things have gone wrong.

This week, try practicing a lament. If there is something in your life that lends itself to a lament, write one and pray it. Share it with others. If this is not a time of loss or confusion with God that is worthy of a lament, think of a time where it would have been appropriate. Write a lament for that time in your life.

A Weak Confession (Joshua 7.20–21)

And Achan answered Joshua, "It is true; I am the one who sinned against the LORD God of Israel. This is what I did: when I saw among the spoil a beautiful mantle from Shinar, and two hundred shekels of silver, and a bar of gold weighing fifty shekels, then I coveted them and took them. They now lie hidden in the ground inside my tent, with the silver underneath."

Background

This passage, like the first one in Joshua, makes us wonder if it is actually a prayer—in this case, a confession. It appears to be so; it begins the phrase "I am the one who sinned…" Yet it lacks much of the language that is usually found in prayers of confession. This is the first confession we have encountered in our study. It is not a good model.

The context of the story is a continuation of the last. After the loss at Ai,[1] Joshua offered a prayer of lament. God told him the loss was a result of the misdeeds of his people. Following a night's sleep, Joshua assembled the tribes of Israel. With care, he works down the hierarchy. He locates the tribe responsible for disobeying God, then the clan, the family, the sub-family, and finally he comes to a man, Achan. Joshua tells Achan to give the glory to God and to confess. He urges him to be honest and not hide anything. Achan, to his credit, confesses that it was he who kept some of the spoils of war. He disobeyed the *herem* order by keeping a beautiful mantle and some silver and gold from Jericho. He knew God had commanded that they be destroyed. He kept them anyway.

Joshua sent men to Achan's tent to verify his story; they find the treasure just as he said. The treasure is laid before Achan and all the people of Israel. Because of his failure to keep the *herem*, he has now become the *herem*—the thing forbidden. His selfish actions have affected the whole community through a loss of a battle and loss of life. He violated the ban; he now becomes the ban. Achan, his wife and children, his tent, his animals, and all their belongings are taken outside the camp. As God ordered, Achan and his family are executed, and all their belongings were all burned. The people raise a heap of stones above the destruction.

Again we find a disturbing harshness in God's judgment. We will leave those questions to other commenta-

---

[1] See the previous chapter.

A Weak Confession (Joshua 7.20–21)

tors and theologians. When we explore the prayer-confession we find it lacking in sincerity and depth, like many other prayers (or not-prayers) in Joshua. Joshua orders Achan to "give glory to God" and to "confess." Nothing in Achan's response gives glory to God, and his confession is little more than "yes, I did it and here are the details." The answer appears almost flippant. Is this what the writer intended us to understand? Or is the writer only moving with speed through a troubling story, and we should not read to much into its brevity?

The context and content of Joshua reveal that it is the former. Throughout the book, the writer shows that the leaders and the people became complacent in their relationship with God. They take His presence (and His blessings) for granted. The confession is not much of a confession. For example, compare it with the confession in 1 Samuel 12.10:

> *"Then they cried to the LORD, and said,*
> *'We have sinned, because we have forsaken*
> *the LORD, and have served the Baals and*
> *the Astartes...'"*

This is a genuine confession, exemplified by the crying and frank admission of sin. That passage continues with the people asking God to forgive them and rescue them. Achan's confession contains no "because," no mention of his forsaking God, and no cry for forgiveness. Achan's refusal to obey God is a danger for Israel; his attitude about it is another danger.

Meaning

What do we learn from this prayer? First, this prayer, and the story around it, emphasized the seriousness of sin. It is not a "mistake." We are not to be flippant about it and think that "God is in the forgiving business; it is no big deal." Sin *is* a "big deal." Whether our actions result in the death of people or only hurt feelings, if we violate God's character and commands it is a serious matter. Like a craftsman who makes a tool to perform a certain function, God has created humans to live and act in certain ways. If we try to use a screwdriver as a hammer, it might work, but we will likely damage the screwdriver and perhaps make a mess of things. It is not its created purpose. If you do it a lot, worse damage can occur. It is likewise with humans. If we live outside our "created purpose," we may be able to function, but it will not be for the best, and we will cause damage—perhaps little at first, but it will worsen if we continue. All sin is serious because it is a violation and a misuse of our created nature. It is contrary to our purpose in life.

Second, and connected to the first: we ought to make sure our confessions are honest and genuine. A confession should be specific and heartfelt, not merely "yes, I did that, and here's how." We should try to realize the depth of pain we cause God, and the damage (or potential damage) we are creating for ourselves and others.

Application

Think about one of your specific sins, whether recent or in the past. Did you confess them (to God and others)?

A Weak Confession (Joshua 7.20–21)

We all tend to be defensive; it is difficult to only confess without offering some justifications. A good practice in confession is to refuse to use words like "but," "however," and, one of the worst, "but he/she did it too!"

Try writing a confession using a recent or past sin. Avoid the words mentioned above. Confess, don't be flippant, and address it with all seriousness. Offer the prayer you have written, out loud. Perhaps you can pray it with someone else. Write down the thoughts you have about confession.

A Failure To Pray
(Joshua 9.14)

So the leaders partook of their provisions, and did not ask direction from the LORD...

Background

This passage mentions prayer, but there is no prayer. Unlike the passages in 1.17 and 7.20–21, where it was not clear if there *was* a prayer or not, here the writer tells us that the leaders *did not pray*.

In the scene prior, Joshua called the people together to hold a solemn ceremony. An altar was built, which followed God's specific directions given to Moses by God and then by Moses to Joshua. When finished, they offered sacrifices upon the altar, again following God's instructions. Despite past failings of Israel and the lack of spiritual leadership, the Israelites are back on track with their faith and practice. Alas, once again, it does not last.

A band of weary travelers appears in the region. Their clothes are old and worn; their food is stale. They tell Joshua that they have come from far away and wished to settle in the land, at least for a while. They had heard rumors of the Israelites victories—they stress that they are not there to cause problems. They propose a covenant and a meal to be shared in honor of that promise. Joshua and the elders agree to the covenant. They will live in peace with these travelers. The scene closes with this ominous sentence: they "did not ask direction from the LORD."

A reader familiar with the book of Joshua might respond with a weary "Oh, no." A reader familiar with cultures of the ancient near east will know that it was normal for *any* community to inquire of their gods during negotiations. One group did not make a covenant with another group without seeking a divine word. Here, the chosen people of God do not even bother to ask advice of Him. If they had, they would have discovered that these travelers were not as they appeared. They were not from far away. They were local inhabitants who had dressed like travelers to deceive the Israelites so that they could keep their land and their lives.

When the Israelites discovered the deception, they were angry. Joshua told them that there was nothing he could do, because, "We have sworn to them by the LORD, the God of Israel, and now we must not touch them" (v19).

The leaders had sworn the oath in the name of God, without asking Him first. (Note that the Israelites have the integrity to keep *this* covenant, but cannot seem to keep God's covenants.)

The short-term result was, perhaps, negligible. Later, there would be problems with foreign influence in faith and practice and worship other gods. God intended the land to be free of such influences. He gave the land to the Israelites so they could live in peace and in concert with God. Because the leaders did not inquire of God, the land

A Failure To Pray (Joshua 9.14)

still had people worshipping other gods and living by other values. It would cost the Israelites in their spiritual life and more.

Meaning

What can we learn about a passage where people should pray, but do not? There have likely been times in our lives where we should have prayed but did not. It is (hopefully) rare that we *intentionally* do not pray. Our reasons for not offering prayer might be that we were too rushed or distracted. We might know that it is a good idea to pray before a major decision or before any important event. God's followers should inquire of God. God's followers make Him a part of their decision-making. Whether He answers or not is irrelevant—we are His children and He is our parent—we talk to him. There may be no answer, and perhaps He is telling us, "do what you prefer, it doesn't matter." Either way, it is the *communication* that is important between parent and child, between the Creator and the created.

When we neglect to pray, it might not be at a low point in our spiritual lives. It may just be that we are finite humans who are sometimes weak and inconsistent. Joshua and his people held a sacrificial service, then immediately ignored God. Likewise, we may be attending worship services, praying, and reading scripture. We may look as if we are following God, and then it appears we forgot. We are weak and easily distracted. It is the reason we need God and the reason why we need constant reminders of who we are, who we follow, and how we must live our lives.

Application

This passage is a reminder that we should always be alert times for times when we can pray. We do not want to be like Joshua and the leaders of Israel, who worship at one moment and go off on their own as if it never happened. Our task is to teach ourselves, when we are busy and distracted, to stop—even for just a moment—and inquire of God. This takes practice; it takes a community of believers holding each other accountable. It may also require some humility and reflection of why we neglect prayer in some circumstances, and to think of ways in which we can avoid it in the future. And, of course, we can pray about our failure of prayer!

A Secularized Prayer (Joshua 10.12)

On the day when the LORD gave the Amorites over to the Israelites, Joshua spoke to the LORD; and he said in the sight of Israel,

"Sun, stand still at Gibeon, and Moon, in the valley of Aijalon."

Background

We have come to the first example of a petitionary prayer in the book of Joshua. Yet, true to form, this petition is not like other petitionary prayers of the Bible. After "Joshua spoke to the Lord," we expect an address to God. Perhaps a praise of His name and then the actual request, followed by some closing address to God. Yet we find that Joshua only says: "Sun, stand still at Gibeon, and Moon, in the valley of Aijalon." It sounds more like an order than a request, and, if it were not for the previous phrase, we would think Joshua was speaking directly to the sun and moon rather than God. A few lines later, we read that "God listened to a man."

Some background sheds light on the prayer (pun intended). Many kings in the region, having heard about the Israelites' alliance with the Gibeonites,[1] formed their own alliance to fight the Israelites. During the battle, as the Israelites are winning, Joshua speaks to God, and the sun and moon "stand still" and "wait." The Israelites defeat their enemies. In spite of their lack of faith (and forgetfulness about prayer), God is still with them.

In the Ancient Near East, it was common for pagan priests and leaders to address celestial objects as gods or goddesses. They believed that those objects were either representations or manifestations of the gods. The Israelites did not follow this view, of course. Celestial objects were creations of God, not representations or manifestations of God. Yet when we read Joshua's words, he speaks like the polytheists who lived in the land. The words are the same words found in a prayer from an ancient collection called the Book of Ishtar.[2] Only the context tells us he is speaking with God.

Meaning

There are four possibilities for understanding this passage. First, Joshua might be *mimicking* the Canaanite religions to dishearten them, by showing them that God commands the heavens. Second, it might be stylistic, using common ancient language in a book about a holy

---

[1] See the previous chapter.
[2] See also 1 Sam 1.18.

A Secularized Prayer (Joshua 10.12)

war. Third, it may be that Joshua has become influenced by the culture around him so that he uses a style and language belonging to the Canaanite religions. (In the context of the rest book of Joshua, this option is tempting.) Finally, it could be that Joshua *did* pray like a pagan, and the writer or later editor added the parts about Joshua "speaking" to God and God "listening" to a human. Most scholars think the last option is the most likely. The narrator wants to show later readers that, despite Joshua's lack of faith, God was still with him and his people, and He had heard the prayer.

What can we glean from this obscure passage? We can use it to check our prayers, based on one of those possible ways of interpreting it. We can examine our prayers and our attitudes towards prayer for secular or cultural influences that might contradict biblical theology and practice. Of course, not all cultural influences are negative. For example, when human rights issues were emphasized by later cultures (pertaining to slavery, for instance), Christian prayer adopted some of the language used by the larger culture. This is quite natural because God is "for" human rights in the sense that he created all people, and all people stand before him on equal ground. It was natural for people of faith to fall in line with such a cultural movement (though not all did, of course).

But cultural influences can be negative. For example, the current Western emphasis on individual "rights" can become an attitude of "no one can tell me what to do" or "if something you say offends me, I can demand you stop." These attitudes run counter to the theological and biblical standard that we are each part of a community created by God. Forbearance for one another and a sense that the community stands above the individual is what He asks of us.

Cultural attitudes can seep into our prayers. Do we pray more often for others to be enlightened, instead of praying for our own patience and understanding? Or perhaps we find ourselves often praying for physical things since materialism is a common characteristic of Western cultures.

Application

The best way to check your prayers is to write them down or record yourself saying them. Analyze what presumptions and attitudes lie behind some of your thoughts, especially in your petitions. Are they in conflict with the cross-centered, sacrificial, God-focused messages of the Bible?

Another way to check your prayers is to argue with yourself about the parts of your prayers—become a devil's advocate (so to speak) for your attitudes. How would you criticize them? Make yourself defend the elements of your prayers on biblical grounds.

Our goal, of course, is to enrich our prayer life, and in that vein, we can find a positive note here. God was with Joshua and the Israelites despite the paucity of their faith or their mixed-up cultural attitudes. As we pray, and even as we work on making our prayers richer and more sound, we can know that God is on our side. Even if our prayers are weak or too influenced by selfishness or secular ideas, God still listens and does what is best for us. I do not have to "get it right" for Him to hear me; I just have to keep talking and learning. What an encouragement!

Blessings
(Joshua 14.13, 22.6–7)

Then Joshua blessed him...

So Joshua blessed them and sent them away...and when Joshua had sent them away to their tents and blessed them...

Background

The last three prayers in the book of Joshua are minor references to prayer-blessings. They are similar to other blessings in the Bible (unlike many other prayers we have encountered in Joshua). All three address the division of the Promised Land among the twelve tribes and others.

Following the previous prayer passage (10.12), the author recounts some battles and the conquest of Canaan (Chapters 11–12). Chapter 13 describes the geography and boundaries of conquered land.

The following chapters recount the official division of the land to each tribe of Israel and to people who helped the Israelites. Before the actual divisions are announced, Caleb requests special treatment. He is described as the only faithful Israelite who acted as a spy in the conquering of the land. He was faithful to God and the people of Israel. Caleb reminds Joshua of this and asks Joshua to give land to his family before the rest of the apportionment. He has a good reason: forty-five years earlier, Moses had promised Caleb that he would have the hill country in Hebron. Joshua pronounces it so, followed by the phrase "Then Joshua blessed him..." and gave his family Hebron. The writer does not tell us the content of the prayer, only that Joshua offered it.

Joshua then distributes the rest of the land. The distribution contains gifts of land to many tribes, families, and people, but there are no blessings mentioned with them. After finishing, Joshua establishes "cities of refuge." These are six cities that will serve as places of asylum for anyone who might be a target of criminal violence or vengeance. Chapter 20 records some special residential and grazing rights to the priests and their families in each of the twelve territories. Even here, there are no blessings or prayers of any kind.

The last group left standing before Joshua are those who live across the Jordan River to the east. These are relatives of the "west bank" Israelites that had fought alongside them to help win the promised land, though they already had their land on the other side. Joshua thanks them for their loyalty and their bravery and exhorts them to stay faithful to God. "So Joshua blessed them and sent them away...and when Joshua had sent them away to their tents and blessed them..." Again, a typical mention of blessings at a time we would expect, though we are not given the words of the blessings.

Blessings (Joshua 14.13, 22.6–7)

Meaning

These are the last reference to prayer in the book of Joshua. We might be disappointed there are not more—and more to them—after all, compare the blessings of Noah to his sons in Genesis 9.25–27 or the blessing that Jacob (Israel) pronounced on the sons of Joseph in Genesis 49.18.

Faithful to the rest of the book, even this scene presents some problems. When the final group left and reached the Jordan River, they built a massive altar before crossing over to their homes. The Israelites heard that they had broken Moses' instructions about having only one central altar (Deut 12.1–14), so they gathered to attack. When they asked how they could commit such sin, the east bank Israelites responded that they did not build a sacrificial altar. It was only a monument. They feared that someday the west-bankers would forget their connection to the east-bankers and deprive them of their rights of inheritance. The east-bankers accept this, and all was well. For now. It will cause problems later, however, and this story serves as a foreshadow.

Application

The final prayers in Joshua do not give us much to draw on for our study. We might use it as a reminder that prayer should be a part of any important event in our lives. These blessings might also serve to remind us that we are not called to give mere lip service to our prayers. While it is surely better to offer a brief (and even shallow) prayer than no prayer at all, we should strive for deeper and more integrated prayers. Can you think of a time when you did not offer prayer during a crucial event, or a time where you sent a friend or family member off on a journey without a blessing? Think of it not as a failure, but as a reminder, like these passages in Joshua, to be more faithful in prayer.

Summary of the Prayers in Joshua

Almost all the prayers in the book of Joshua provide negative examples. The people neglected to pray, and when they do pray, the prayers are often shallow, perfunctory, or self-focused. This depiction of prayer may be some foreshadowing by the author. Though the book of Joshua recounts the battle for the Promised Land, and God's promise fulfilled, the people do not always follow God's orders, which sometimes leads to dire consequences. God was trying to protect His people from negative influences, but their failure to follow His words come back to haunt them. Perhaps the writer is showing us that the lack of attention to sincere and vibrant prayer is part of the problem.

Of the eight prayers in Joshua, only the blessings (14.13, 22.6–7) appear to match blessings in the rest of the Bible. Even these are just mentions of blessings. There is a confession that does not sound like a much of a confession, a prayer-vow turns out to be ill-informed, the lament is self-centered and blind to reality, a prayer that may not be a prayer at all, and a place where the Israelites and their leaders should have prayed, but did not. The one petition sounds like a pagan petition to the sun and moon (though it may be on purpose to razz the enemy).

If it was the intent of the author to use prayer as another way of showing us the failures of the Israelites, then the lesson for us is this: prayer, and our attitude towards it, should not be taken lightly.

Conclusion

The books of Genesis, Exodus, Leviticus, Numbers, Deuteronomy, and Joshua form a literary whole in many ways. In fact, most scholars believe these six books were mostly written or heavily edited by the same person or group.

The first eleven chapters are a theological approach to Creation and humans, focusing on the purpose of both. The rest of the writings deal with God's work through individuals, families, and a nation. It traces their beginnings, their triumphs and difficulties, their enslavement and deliverance—up to the moment where they enter the Promised Land and begin to settle. So it is not just the literary character that binds the six together, the content, too, forms a cohesive collection. The books following Joshua deal with Israel as they progress from a confederation of tribes to a monarchy, to a divided kingdom, and to destruction and exile. We will study the prayers of those books in the next volume of this series, *Praying Through the Bible (Volume 2: Judges–2 Samuel)*.

Prayer, as we have seen, plays a significant role in Genesis through Joshua. Having worked through every prayer passage in these five books, you may wonder where to go from here. We have learned a lot, yet have hardly made a dent in the Bible.

I suggest you keep working with what you have learned. Work through this book again, focusing on individual aspects of each passage. Or you could share the book with a church or a Bible study group.

Spend some time examining only one type of prayer. Use the Appendix and choose one of the prayer types to work through the chapters listed. By studying one type of prayer throughout the six books, rather working through them in order, you will gain insights into that prayer type that might otherwise be missed.

As noted in the Introduction, prayer is primarily about relationship. Like any relationship, it requires learning, listening, practice, re-evaluating, and humility. But it is the journey that matters, not the destination. Enjoy that journey. With the Apostle Paul, I urge to you to "...pray in all things, devote yourselves to prayer, keeping alert in it with thanksgiving."

Most of all, be joyful in prayer, which is part of the gift of relationship given to you by your Creator.

Appendix
Prayers by Category

The following is a list of every prayer in each of the nine categories: blessings, confession and repentance, curses, intercession, lament, petition, praise, thanksgiving, and prayer-Vow. Prayer passages that contain more than one type are listed in both.

Blessings

Noah's Blessings and Curses (Gen 9.25-27)
Melchizedek Blesses Abram (Gen 14.19-20)
A Chain of Prayers: Petition-Thanksgiving-Blessing
    (Gen 24.12-14, 27, 42-44, 48, 52, 60)
A Blessing Wrought in Deception (Gen 27.7, 12–13,
    27–29; 28.2-4)
Israel Blesses the Sons of Joseph (Gen 48.15-16, 20)
Jethro Blesses the Lord (Exod 18.10)
Aaron Blesses the People (Lev 9.22)
The Lord Bless You and Keep You (Num 6.24-26)
Praying for More (Deut 1.11)
Do Not Forget (Deut 8.10) 201
A Prayer for First Fruits (Deut 26.13-15)
Four Kinds of Blessings (Deut 33.6-29)

Blessings (Joshua 14.13, 22.6–7)

Confession and Repentance

A Weak Confession (Josh 7.20-21)

Curses

Noah's Blessings and Curses (Gen 9.25-27)
A Blessing Wrought in Deception (Gen 27.7, 12–13, 27–29; 28.2-4)
A Curse-Prayer (Joshua 6.26)

Intercession

Abraham Intercedes for Abimelech (Gen 20.7, 17)
Intercession and Petition for a Child (Gen 25.21, 22)
Israel's Prayer for his Son's Success (Gen 43.14)
Moses Offers a Prayer on Behalf of Pharaoh (Exod 8.8-9, 12)
Moses Prays Again for the Pharaoh (Exod 9.28-29, 33)
Moses Offers a Third Prayer for the Pharaoh (Exod 10.17-18)
The Art of Complaining (Num 11.2)
Prayers, Whiners, and Snakes (Num 21.7)
Extreme Prayer (Deut 9.26-29)
A Not-Prayer (Joshua 1.17)

Appendix Prayers by Category

Lament

Hagar's Lament and Petition (Gen 21.16)
A Lament (Joshua 7.7–9)

Petition

The Personal Name of God (Gen 4.26)
Hagar's Lament and Petition (Gen 21.16)
A Chain of Prayers: Petition-Thanksgiving-Blessing
 (Gen 24.12-14, 27, 42-44, 48, 52, 60)
Intercession and Petition for a Child (Gen 25.21, 22)
Waiting in Prayer (Gen 30.17-22)
Jacob's Petition for Safety (Gen 32.9-12)
The Israelites Cry Out for Help (Exod 2.23)
The Song of the Ark (Num 10.35-36)
A Failure To Pray (Joshua 9.14)
A Secularized Prayer (Joshua 10.12)

Praise

A Prayer-Hymn of Praise (Exod 15.1-18)
Miriam and the Women Praise God (Exod 15.21)
Perspective in Fear (Deut 3.24-25)

Thanksgiving

A Chain of Prayers: Petition-Thanksgiving-Blessing
 (Gen 24.12-14, 27, 42-44, 48, 52, 60)

Praying Through the Bible (Volume 1: Gen–Josh)

A Prayer-Hymn of Praise (Exod 15.1-18)
Miriam and the Women Praise God (Exod 15.21)

Prayer-Vow

Jacob's Vow (Gen 28.20-22)
A Brief Prayer of Trust in God by Jacob (Gen 49.18)
Men, Daughters, Wives and Vows (Num 30)

ABOUT THE AUTHOR

Markus McDowell is a writer, editor, and researcher, and has lectured at various universities in the US, Europe, and the UK. He has a Ph.D. from Fuller Theological Seminary and a law degree from the University of London, and is the author of *Prayers of Jewish Women: Studies of Patterns of Prayer in the Second Temple Period*, *Prayer in the Ancient Stoic Tradition*, and *Epistolary Prayer in the Apostolic Fathers*.

If you wish to receive notice of publication of other volumes in the *Praying Through the Bible* series, and for notification of other books and articles by Markus McDowell, visit the websites below:

>Mailing list http://eepurl.com/bGVLrL

>Facebook https://www.facebook.com/MarkusMcDowellAuthor/

>Website www.markusmcdowell.com

www.ingramcontent.com/pod-product-compliance
Lightning Source LLC
Chambersburg PA
CBHW021140080526
44588CB00008B/139